Sunset

Fresh Ways with
Chicken

By the Editors of Sunset Books and Sunset Magazine

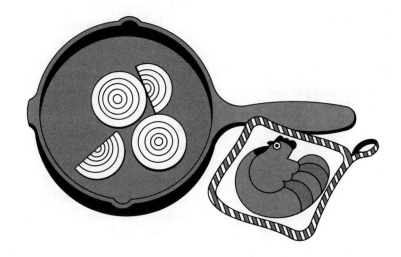

Lane Publishing Co. · Menlo Park, California

Research & Text: **Elaine Johnson**

Coordinating Editor: **Suzanne N. Mathison**

Special Consultant: **Joan Griffiths**

Design: **Joe di Chiarro**

Illustrations: **H. Tom Kamifuji**
Sally Shimizu

Photo Stylist: **Lynne B. Morrall**

Food Stylist: **Cynthia Scheer**

Photographers: Victor Budnik, pages 2, 6, 11, 14, 19, 22, 27, 30, 51, 54, 59, 67, 70; **Michael Lamotte,** page 78; **Darrow M. Watt,** page 62; **Nikolay Zurek,** page 75.

Cover: A medley of garden-fresh vegetables surrounds succulent, golden brown chicken in this colorful presentation. The recipe for Harvest Chicken with Vegetables & Roasted Potatoes is on page 8. Photograph by Darrow M. Watt. Cover design by Lynne B. Morrall.

For every occasion, for every taste

Versatile and economical, good-tasting and nutritious, chicken is always a perfect choice. In this book, you'll discover a wealth of fresh ideas for chicken cookery—from holiday classics to everyday fare, from formal dinner offerings to simple snacks and appetizers.

Chicken not only combines well with other ingredients, but also lends itself to a number of different cooking methods. No matter how you like to cook chicken—in the oven, in a frying pan, on the barbecue, or in a kettle—you can choose from a wide variety of recipes. You'll also find recipes for other types of poultry, including turkey, duck, game hens, and goose. And for poultry that's already cooked, we offer a selection of salads, sandwiches, and casseroles.

Whether you're a beginner or an experienced cook, you'll appreciate the tips on buying, storing, and preparing poultry, along with the step-by-step illustrations of cutting and carving techniques.

For their generosity in sharing props for use in our photographs, we're grateful to House of Today, Livingston's, Menlo Park Hardware Co., The Minimal Space, Peck's of Burlingame, Rorke's, S. Christian of Copenhagen Inc., William Ober Co., and Williams-Sonoma. We also extend special thanks to Rebecca La Brum for her editing of the manuscript.

Editor, Sunset Books: David E. Clark
First printing January 1986

Contents

Morsels of marinated chicken grilled alongside papaya and pine-apple make a tropical treat: Chicken & Fruit Kebabs (page 38).

Oven Feasts

Chicken roasted, broiled & baked

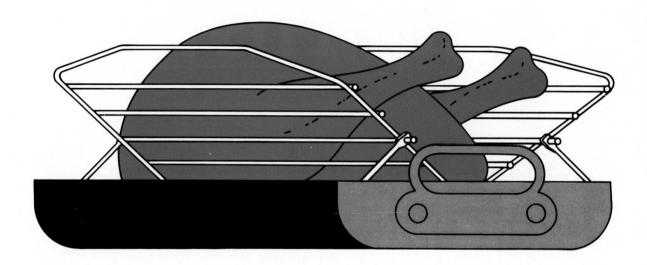

few foods are as appealing and satisfying as succulent, golden brown chicken, hot from the oven. There's splendid variety in oven cooking, too—roasted birds filled with savory stuffings, broiled chicken enhanced with marinades, and baked chicken plain or fancy.

Experienced cooks as well as novices will enjoy our selection of roast chicken recipes. Some are extra-easy—Simple Herb Chicken, for example. Others, such as Roast Chicken with Hazelnut Wild Rice Stuffing, are fancier fare that's perfect for company. For pointers to success with any roast chicken, turn to page 13; you'll find tips on techniques as well as a chart of roasting temperatures and times.

If you plan to do much roasting, it pays to have the right equipment. A meat thermometer is an invaluable aid, letting you check doneness at a glance. You might also want to invest in a V-shaped or vertical roasting rack; these support poultry better than conventional flat racks and provide more even cooking.

If you're looking for recipes that are especially quick to cook, choose broiled chicken. The broiler's intense heat seals in juices in minutes, keeping meat moist while skin turns brown and crisp. Many of these recipes also offer make-ahead ease. Broiled Chicken with Fresh Peaches, for example, can marinate for as little as 2 hours or as long as overnight, depending on your schedule.

Among our baked chicken recipes, you'll find good choices for every occasion. Some are seasoned with spices or accented with fruit; others feature glazes or crisp, crunchy coatings. Use a cut-up bird, or just highlight your favorite part—thighs, drumsticks, breasts, or wings.

Roast Chicken à la Provençale

From sun-bathed southern France comes this elegant recipe, perfect for a special occasion.

> 5 to 6-pound roasting chicken
> Swiss Chard Stuffing (recipe follows)
> Provençale Tomato Sauce (recipe follows)

Remove chicken neck and giblets. Set liver aside for use in stuffing; reserve neck and remaining giblets for other uses, if desired. Discard lumps of fat. Rinse chicken inside and out; pat dry.

Prepare Swiss Chard Stuffing. Stuff and truss chicken; then bend wings akimbo (see page 65).

Place chicken, breast down, on a rack in a shallow roasting pan. Roast, uncovered, in a 350° oven for 1 hour. Turn chicken over and continue to roast until a meat thermometer inserted in thickest portion of thigh (not touching bone) registers 185°F or until meat near thighbone is no longer pink when slashed (1 to 1¼ more hours).

Meanwhile, prepare sauce; pass at the table to top stuffing and meat. Makes 6 or 7 servings.

Swiss Chard Stuffing. Thoroughly rinse about 1 pound **Swiss chard.** Cut white stems crosswise into ¼-inch slices, then coarsely chop leaves; set stems and leaves aside separately.

Heat ¼ cup **olive oil** or salad oil in a wide frying pan over medium heat. Add ¼ cup **pine nuts** and cook, stirring, until golden; lift out and set aside. Add 1 medium-size **onion** (chopped), chard stems, and 1 clove **garlic** (minced or pressed). Cover and cook until chard is tender when pierced (about 5 minutes). Chop **chicken liver** and add to chard mixture; cook, stirring, until liver is no longer pink. Stir in chard leaves, cover, and cook until leaves are wilted (about 4 more minutes). Remove from heat; mix in pine nuts, ¾ cup **cooked rice,** ¼ cup grated **Parmesan cheese,** and ¾ teaspoon **dry rosemary.** Season to taste with **salt** and **pepper.** Let cool. Makes 4 cups.

Provençale Tomato Sauce. Heat ¼ cup **olive oil** or salad oil in a 3-quart pan over medium heat. Add 1 large **onion,** chopped; cook, stirring, until soft. Stir in 1 can (14½ oz.) **pear-shaped tomatoes** (break up with a spoon) and their liquid; ¼ cup **dry white wine;** ¼ cup **regular-strength chicken broth,** homemade (page 53) or purchased; 1 clove **garlic** (minced or pressed); ¾ teaspoon *each* **dry rosemary** and crushed **fennel seeds;** one ½ by 2-inch strip **orange peel;** 1 **bay leaf;** and ½ teaspoon **sugar.** Bring to a boil; then reduce heat and simmer, uncovered, until almost all liquid has evaporated (about 45 minutes). Remove and discard bay leaf and orange peel; season sauce to taste with **salt** and **pepper.** Stir in 12 to 16 **pitted ripe olives.** If made ahead, cover and refrigerate until next day; reheat just before serving.

Cheese-crusted Chicken with Cream

This roast chicken dish has a special yet simple finishing touch. You quarter the cooked chicken and sprinkle the pieces with Swiss cheese, then broil them briefly to develop an appetizing crust. A rich, delicate sauce made from the pan juices, cream, mustard, and more cheese accompanies each serving.

> 3½ to 4-pound whole frying chicken
> About 1 tablespoon butter or margarine, melted
> 1¼ cups (5 oz.) shredded Gruyère or Swiss cheese
> 1 tablespoon Dijon mustard
> About ¾ cup whipping cream
> Watercress

Remove chicken neck and giblets; reserve for other uses, if desired. Discard lumps of fat. Rinse chicken inside and out, then pat dry. Bend wings akimbo as shown on page 65. Brush skin with butter. Place chicken, breast down, on a rack in a shallow roasting pan. Roast, uncovered, in a 375° oven for 30 minutes; then turn over and continue to roast until a meat thermometer inserted in thickest part of thigh (not touching bone) registers 185°F or until meat near thighbone is no longer pink when slashed (30 to 45 more minutes).

Using poultry shears or a knife, cut chicken into quarters. Arrange pieces, skin side up and slightly apart, in a shallow ovenproof serving dish. Sprinkle with ¾ cup of the cheese. Return to oven and turn off heat.

Skim and discard fat from pan drippings. Stir in mustard and ¾ cup of the cream; bring to a boil over high heat and boil, stirring, until shiny bubbles form (3 to 4 minutes). Remove from heat, add remaining ½ cup cheese, and stir until cheese is melted and sauce is smooth (if necessary, thin sauce with a little more cream). Keep sauce warm.

Broil chicken 4 to 5 inches below heat until cheese is bubbly (about 1 minute). Pour sauce around chicken; garnish with watercress. Makes 4 servings.

In true Oriental fashion, Peking-style Chicken (facing page) offers a pleasing contrast of flavors and textures. Flour tortillas spread with spicy-sweet hoisin wrap up the soy-marinated meat, crunchy onions, and nippy cilantro.

Chicken Laurel

Bay leaves, onion slices, and chunks of orange are tucked inside this chicken before roasting to give the meat a delicate aroma. The rich-tasting sauce features three kinds of orange flavoring: juice, peel, and liqueur.

    5 to 6-pound roasting chicken
1   medium-size onion, sliced
1   large orange (unpeeled), cut into chunks
6   fresh bay leaves (or 3 or 4 dry bay leaves)
4   tablespoons butter or margarine
    About 1½ pounds asparagus
½   teaspoon grated orange peel
½   cup orange juice
¼   cup orange-flavored liqueur
1   or 2 large oranges, peeled, white membrane removed, and sliced
    Small cluster of fresh bay leaves (optional)

Remove chicken neck and giblets; reserve for other uses, if desired. Discard lumps of fat. Rinse chicken inside and out; pat dry. Fill neck cavity and body cavity with onion, orange chunks, and the 6 bay leaves. Truss, then bend wings akimbo (see page 65).

Place chicken, breast down, on a rack in a shallow roasting pan. Roast, uncovered, in a 350° oven for 30 minutes. Rub skin with 1 tablespoon of the butter. Roast for 30 more minutes, then turn chicken over and rub with 1 more tablespoon butter. Continue to roast until a meat thermometer inserted in thickest portion of thigh (not touching bone) registers 185°F or until meat near thighbone is no longer pink when slashed (1 to 1¼ more hours).

Remove and discard onion, orange chunks, and bay leaves from chicken cavities. Protecting your hands, tip chicken to drain juices from body into roasting pan; transfer chicken to a platter and keep warm.

Snap off and discard tough ends of asparagus; rinse stalks well. Bring 1 inch of water to a boil in a wide frying pan over high heat. Add asparagus; reduce heat, cover, and simmer until tender when pierced (7 to 10 minutes).

Meanwhile, skim and discard fat from pan drippings. Add orange peel and orange juice; bring to a boil over medium heat, stirring to scrape browned bits free. Add remaining 2 tablespoons butter and stir until melted. Pour liqueur into a small, deep pan; heat over medium heat until bubbly, then ignite (not beneath a vent or fan). Stir into sauce. Pour sauce into a serving bowl.

Arrange asparagus on platter around chicken; garnish with orange slices and, if desired, a small cluster of fresh bay leaves. Pass orange sauce at the table to spoon over chicken. Makes 6 or 7 servings.

Peking-style Chicken

(Pictured on facing page)

In this recipe reminiscent of Peking duck, crisply roasted chicken halves—one for each diner—take the place of duck; warmed flour tortillas stand in for the traditional steamed Mandarin pancakes.

2   whole frying chickens (2½ lbs. *each*)
4   quarts water
¼   teaspoon pepper
½   teaspoon *each* ground cinnamon and ginger
1   tablespoon *each* firmly packed brown sugar and vinegar
2   teaspoons soy sauce
12 flour tortillas, *each* about 8 inches in diameter
    Hoisin or Chinese plum sauce
2   bunches green onions (including tops), cut into 2-inch-long slivers
    Fresh cilantro (coriander) sprigs

Remove chicken necks and giblets; reserve for other uses, if desired. Discard lumps of fat. Using poultry shears or a knife, cut each chicken in half lengthwise; then rinse halves and pat dry. In a large pan, bring water to a boil over high heat. Remove pan from heat; plunge chicken into water. Let stand for 1 minute; lift out and pat very dry.

In a small bowl, combine pepper, cinnamon, ginger, sugar, vinegar, and soy; brush over skin sides of chicken halves. Place chicken in a large bowl; cover and refrigerate for 4 to 8 hours.

Lift chicken from bowl and place, skin side up, on a rack in a large, shallow roasting pan. Roast, uncovered, in a 400° oven until skin is richly browned and crisp and meat near thighbone is no longer pink when slashed (40 to 45 minutes).

Meanwhile, cut tortillas in half and divide into 2 equal stacks; wrap each stack in foil. Place in oven 15 minutes before chicken is done.

When chicken is done, turn off oven; place one chicken half on each of 4 dinner plates. Unwrap one stack of tortillas, re-wrap in a napkin, and bring to the table (leave second stack in oven until needed). To eat, top a tortilla with hoisin, onions, and cilantro; carve off pieces of chicken, wrap in tortilla, and eat out of hand. Makes 4 servings.

Chicken with Bacon

Bacon slices laid over the breast during roasting give chicken a pleasantly smoky flavor.

>   3 to 3½-pound whole frying chicken
>   Salt, pepper, and garlic powder
>   2 tablespoons butter or margarine
> 1½ cups dry white wine
>   1 tablespoon finely chopped parsley
>   ½ teaspoon *each* thyme leaves, rubbed sage, and dry rosemary
>   4 slices bacon
>   2 teaspoons *each* cornstarch and water
>   Hot cooked rice

Remove chicken neck and giblets; reserve for other uses, if desired. Discard lumps of fat. Rinse chicken inside and out, then pat dry. Sprinkle body cavity lightly with salt, pepper, and garlic powder. Truss chicken and bend wings akimbo (see page 65); then place, breast down, on a rack in a shallow roasting pan.

Roast, uncovered, in a 375° oven for 15 minutes. Meanwhile, melt butter in a small pan over medium heat; stir in wine, parsley, thyme, sage, and rosemary. Remove from heat. Brush some of the wine mixture over chicken and roast for 15 more minutes, then baste again.

Turn chicken over and arrange bacon on top. Continue to roast, basting often with wine mixture, until a meat thermometer inserted in thickest part of thigh (not touching bone) registers 185°F or until meat near thighbone is no longer pink when slashed (about 30 more minutes).

Transfer chicken to a platter; keep warm. Skim and discard fat from pan drippings. Stir together cornstarch and water, then add to drippings and cook over high heat, stirring, until bubbly and thickened. Pass sauce at the table to spoon over chicken and rice. Makes about 4 servings.

Harvest Chicken with Vegetables & Roasted Potatoes

(Pictured on front cover)

Celebrate an abundant fresh vegetable harvest with this colorful, extra-easy chicken dinner. Potatoes, carrots, bell peppers, two kinds of squash, and cherry tomatoes roast alongside the chicken.

>   4 to 6 red thin-skinned potatoes, *each* 2 to 3 inches in diameter
>   3½ to 4-pound whole frying chicken
>   3 large carrots, cut into 1½-inch chunks
>   4 small pattypan squash
>   3 medium-size crookneck squash, cut into 1½-inch chunks
>   2 large red or green bell peppers, seeded and cut into eighths
>   2 cloves garlic, quartered
>   1 large onion, quartered
> 10 fresh rosemary sprigs (*each* about 6 inches long) or 1 teaspoon dry rosemary
>   6 to 8 cherry tomatoes, stemmed

Pierce potatoes in several places and set on rack in oven as it preheats to 375°.

Remove chicken neck and giblets; reserve for other uses, if desired. Discard lumps of fat. Rinse chicken inside and out, then pat dry. Place, breast down, in a shallow roasting pan (not on a rack). Arrange carrots, pattypan squash, crookneck squash, bell peppers, garlic, and onion around chicken. Lay 4 of the rosemary sprigs on vegetables (or sprinkle with all the dry rosemary).

Roast chicken and vegetables, uncovered, for 30 minutes; stir vegetables occasionally. Turn chicken over and continue to roast until a meat thermometer inserted in thickest portion of thigh (not touching bone) registers 185°F or until meat near thighbone is no longer pink when slashed (30 to 45 more minutes). Add tomatoes during last 10 minutes of cooking.

Transfer chicken to a large platter; carefully lift vegetables from pan with a slotted spoon and mound alongside chicken. Arrange remaining 6 rosemary sprigs around chicken. Skim and discard fat from pan juices; spoon juices over vegetables. Serve potatoes separately. Makes 4 or 5 servings.

Roast Chicken with Hazelnut Wild Rice Stuffing

Wild rice stuffing sparked with crunchy hazelnuts and bits of Italian sausage fills this festive bird. A simple baste of butter and red currant jelly gives the skin a sweet, shiny glaze.

>   5 to 6-pound roasting chicken
>   Hazelnut Wild Rice Stuffing (recipe follows)
>   ½ cup (¼ lb.) butter or margarine
>   2 tablespoons red currant jelly

Remove chicken neck and giblets; reserve for other uses, if desired. Discard lumps of fat. Rinse chicken inside and out; pat dry. Prepare stuffing; stuff and truss chicken, then bend wings akimbo (see page 65). Spoon leftover stuffing into a greased baking dish and bake, covered, during the last 30 minutes of roasting time.

Place chicken, breast down, on a rack in a shallow roasting pan. Roast, uncovered, in a 350° oven for 45 minutes. Meanwhile, melt butter in a small pan over medium heat; add jelly and stir until smooth. Remove from heat. Brush some of the jelly mixture over chicken and roast for 15 more minutes; then turn chicken over. Continue to roast, basting often with jelly mixture, until a meat thermometer inserted in thickest part of thigh (not touching bone) registers 185°F or until meat near thighbone is no longer pink when slashed (1 to 1¼ more hours). Makes 6 or 7 servings.

Hazelnut Wild Rice Stuffing. Into a 2 to 3-quart pan, pour 2 cups **regular-strength chicken broth,** homemade (page 53) or purchased. Bring to a boil; then stir in 1 cup **wild rice.** Reduce heat, cover, and simmer until rice is *al dente* (about 45 minutes).

While rice cooks, discard casings from ½ pound **mild Italian sausage** and crumble meat into a wide frying pan. Add ½ cup chopped **hazelnuts** (filberts) and 1 medium-size **onion,** chopped. Cook over medium heat, stirring, until meat is browned and onion is soft (10 to 15 minutes). Add ¼ cup **brandy** and cook, stirring, until almost all liquid has evaporated (about 1 minute). Stir sausage mixture into cooked rice. Season to taste with **salt** and **pepper.** Let cool. Makes about 4 cups.

Roast Chicken with Prune Plums

Summer's prune plums lend color and flavor appeal to simple roasted chicken. With cooking, the purple skins turn a bright ruby red.

> 3½ to 4-pound **whole frying chicken**
> 12 large firm-ripe **prune plums,** halved and pitted
> ½ cup **port wine** or **apple juice**
> ½ cup **regular-strength chicken broth,** homemade (page 53) or purchased
> ¼ teaspoon **ground ginger**
> ⅓ cup **butter** or **margarine**

Remove chicken neck and giblets; reserve for other uses, if desired. Discard lumps of fat. Rinse chicken inside and out, then pat dry. Place, breast down, on a rack in a shallow roasting pan. Roast, uncovered, in a 375° oven for 30 minutes. Turn chicken over and roast for 20 more minutes.

Add plums to pan, turning fruit in drippings to coat. Continue to roast, turning plums once, until a meat thermometer inserted in thickest part of thigh (not touching bone) registers 185°F or until meat near thighbone is no longer pink when slashed (10 to 25 more minutes).

Transfer chicken to a platter and surround with plums; keep warm. Skim and discard fat from pan drippings. Add port, broth, and ginger to pan. Place over high heat; boil, stirring to scrape browned particles free, until reduced to ½ cup. Reduce heat to low. Add butter and stir until blended. Pass sauce at the table. Makes 4 or 5 servings.

Simple Herb Chicken

What could be simpler or better than roasted chicken with herbs and garlic? Offer Dijon mustard as a piquant accompaniment to the meat.

> 3½ to 4-pound **whole frying chicken**
> **Salt and pepper**
> 4 fresh **rosemary sprigs** (*each* about 6 inches long) or 1 teaspoon dry **rosemary**
> 1 bunch **parsley,** rinsed well
> 6 to 8 cloves **garlic,** quartered

Remove chicken neck and giblets; reserve for other uses, if desired. Discard lumps of fat. Rinse chicken inside and out, then pat dry. Lightly sprinkle neck cavity and body cavity with salt and pepper. Place 2 of the rosemary sprigs in body cavity (or sprinkle cavity with ½ teaspoon of the dry rosemary); then stuff in most of the parsley. Stuff remaining parsley into neck cavity. Rub a few pieces of the garlic over skin, then insert all garlic in body cavity.

Truss chicken as shown on page 65, but do not bend wings akimbo. Instead, place one of the remaining 2 rosemary sprigs under each wing, then tie wings to body with cotton string. (If using dry rosemary, just rub remaining ½ teaspoon over skin.) Rub skin with pepper.

Place chicken, breast down, on a rack in a shallow roasting pan. Roast, uncovered, in a 375° oven for 30 minutes. Turn chicken over and continue to roast until a meat thermometer inserted in thickest portion of thigh (not touching bone) registers 185°F or until meat near thighbone is no longer pink when slashed (30 to 45 more minutes). Makes 4 or 5 servings.

Broiled Chicken with Fresh Peaches

(Pictured on facing page)

A raspberry vinegar marinade gives this broiled chicken its subtle fruitiness. Fresh, juicy peaches dunked in the same marinade broil alongside the chicken; you might serve a tossed green salad and bread sticks as accompaniments.

> 3 to 3½-pound frying chicken, cut up
> ½ cup raspberry vinegar or red wine vinegar
> ½ cup finely chopped fresh basil
> 2 tablespoons salad oil
> 4 firm-ripe peaches or nectarines, *each* about 2 inches in diameter
> Salt and pepper

Reserve chicken neck and giblets for other uses, if desired. Rinse chicken and pat dry.

In a large bowl, combine vinegar, basil, and oil. Add chicken; turn to coat with marinade. Cover and let stand for 2 hours, turning frequently. (Or refrigerate until next day, turning occasionally.)

Lift chicken from marinade (reserve marinade); arrange, skin side down, on a rack in a broiler pan. Broil 4 to 5 inches below heat for 20 minutes, turning chicken as needed to brown evenly.

Meanwhile, peel peaches, cut in half, and pit (if using nectarines, do not peel.) Coat with marinade to prevent darkening, then arrange on rack with chicken. Continue to broil, turning peaches once, until meat near thighbone is no longer pink when slashed and peaches are hot throughout (about 10 more minutes). Season to taste with salt and pepper. Makes about 4 servings.

Teriyaki Chicken Wings

Teriyaki sauce is both marinade and baste for these chicken wings. Complete the menu with rice, stir-fried vegetables, and almond cookies.

> Teriyaki Sauce (recipe follows)
> 3 pounds chicken wings (about 16), rinsed and patted dry
> 2 green onions (including tops), thinly sliced

Prepare Teriyaki Sauce. Cut tips off chicken wings and reserve for other uses, if desired; then stir wings into sauce. Cover and refrigerate for 3 to 4 hours, stirring several times.

Lift wings from sauce (reserve sauce); arrange on a rack in a broiler pan. Drizzle with half the sauce, then broil about 6 inches below heat until golden (about 15 minutes). Turn wings over, drizzle with remaining sauce, and continue to broil until meat is no longer pink when slashed in thickest part (8 to 10 more minutes). Garnish with onions. Makes 3 or 4 servings.

Teriyaki Sauce. In a wide frying pan, combine ¼ cup **sesame seeds** and 3 tablespoons **salad oil;** cook over medium-low heat, stirring occasionally, just until seeds are golden (about 4 minutes). Let cool briefly, then pour into a large bowl. Stir in ¼ cup **soy sauce;** 2 tablespoons firmly packed **brown sugar;** 1 tablespoon **dry sherry;** 2 to 3 teaspoons minced **fresh ginger;** ¼ teaspoon **pepper;** 2 **green onions** (including tops), thinly sliced; and 2 cloves **garlic,** minced or pressed.

Lemony Broiled Chicken

This simple-to-prepare recipe from Lebanon will delight you with its marvelous aroma and lemony, spicy-sweet flavor. For a Greek version of the recipe, using a whole bird on the barbecue, see Mediterranean Fruited Chicken, page 36.

> 3 to 3½-pound frying chicken, quartered
> 3 tablespoons olive oil or salad oil
> ¼ cup fresh lemon juice
> ¾ teaspoon salt
> 1 teaspoon oregano leaves
> ½ teaspoon *each* pepper and ground cinnamon

Reserve chicken neck and giblets for other uses, if desired. Rinse chicken and pat dry.

In a 9 by 13-inch baking pan, stir together oil, lemon juice, salt, oregano, pepper, and cinnamon. Place chicken in marinade; turn to coat both sides. Cover and let stand for 30 minutes, turning occasionally.

Lift chicken from marinade (reserve marinade) and place, skin side down, on a rack in a broiler pan. Broil 6 to 8 inches below heat for 15 minutes, basting once or twice with marinade. Turn chicken over; continue to broil, basting several more times with marinade, until meat near thighbone is no longer pink when slashed (15 to 20 more minutes). Makes 4 servings.

Rosy ripe peaches and basil-flecked chicken combine for a fresh-tasting summertime supper. Offer Broiled Chicken with Fresh Peaches (facing page) with crisp bread sticks and a semi-fruity white wine.

11

Broil-Bake Crispy Chicken

For extra-crisp skin and tender, flavorful meat, try this two-step cooking technique: first broil herb-seasoned chicken pieces, then bake over boiling water in a hot oven.

> **3 to 3½-pound frying chicken, cut up; or 6 whole chicken legs, thighs attached (about 3 lbs. *total*)**
>
> **Seasoned salt, garlic powder, and thyme leaves**
>
> **Boiling water**

Reserve chicken neck and giblets for other uses, if desired. Rinse chicken pieces and pat dry, then sprinkle lightly on all sides with seasoned salt, garlic powder, and thyme. Arrange, skin side down, on a rack in a broiler pan. Broil 4 to 6 inches below heat until lightly browned (about 10 minutes).

Remove broiler pan from oven, move oven rack to center of oven, and reset oven to 500°. Turn chicken pieces over. Return pan to oven; pour boiling water into pan under chicken to a depth of ½ inch.

Bake until chicken is well browned and meat near thighbone is no longer pink when slashed (20 to 25 minutes). Makes about 4 servings.

Broiled Chicken with Herb Butter

Seasoned butter tucked beneath the skin keeps this chicken moist and gives it an herb-lemon flavor.

> **3 tablespoons butter or margarine, softened**
> **3 tablespoons minced shallots or onion**
> **½ teaspoon *each* thyme leaves and rubbed sage**
> **1 teaspoon dry tarragon**
> **¼ teaspoon *each* salt and pepper**
> **1½ teaspoons grated lemon peel**
> **3 to 3½-pound frying chicken, quartered**
> **¼ cup dry white wine or ¼ cup regular-strength chicken broth, homemade (page 53) or purchased**

In a small pan, thoroughly combine butter, shallots, thyme, sage, tarragon, salt, pepper, and lemon peel. Set aside.

Reserve chicken neck and giblets for other uses, if desired. Rinse chicken and pat dry. With a sharp knife, cut small slits in skin over breasts, thighs, and meaty part of wings. Push small

amounts of butter mixture through slits between skin and flesh, using about ¾ of the butter mixture and dividing it evenly among chicken quarters.

Melt remaining butter mixture over low heat and stir in wine. Remove from heat. Arrange chicken quarters, skin side down, on a rack in a broiler pan. Broil 6 to 8 inches below heat for 15 minutes, brushing several times with butter mixture. Turn chicken over and continue to broil, brushing occasionally with butter mixture, until meat near thighbone is no longer pink when slashed (15 to 20 more minutes). Makes 4 servings.

Chicken Satay

Popular throughout Southeast Asia, *satay*—chunks of meat that are skewered, then grilled—makes a delicious appetizer or entrée.

> **1 clove garlic, minced or pressed**
> **2 tablespoons soy sauce**
> **1 tablespoon salad oil**
> **1 teaspoon *each* ground cumin and coriander**
> **2 whole chicken breasts (about 1 lb. *each*), skinned, boned, and split (see page 93)**
> **Basting Sauce (recipe follows)**
> **Peanut Sauce (recipe follows)**

In a bowl, stir together garlic, soy, oil, cumin, and coriander. Rinse chicken and pat dry, then cut into ¾-inch cubes. Add to marinade and stir to coat evenly. Cover and refrigerate for 1½ to 2 hours.

Meanwhile, prepare Basting Sauce and Peanut Sauce; set aside.

Thread 4 or 5 cubes of chicken on each of 14 to 16 small bamboo skewers. Place on a rack in a large broiler pan; brush with half the Basting Sauce. Broil 4 to 6 inches below heat for 3 to 4 minutes; turn over, brush with remaining Basting Sauce, and continue to broil until meat is no longer pink when slashed (3 to 4 more minutes). Serve with Peanut Sauce for dipping. Makes about 8 appetizer servings or 4 main-dish servings.

Basting Sauce. In a bowl, stir together 3 tablespoons **lemon juice**, 2 tablespoons **soy sauce**, and ¼ teaspoon *each* **ground cumin** and **ground coriander**.

Peanut Sauce. In a small pan, combine 1 cup **water**, ⅔ cup **creamy or crunchy peanut butter**, and 2 cloves **garlic**, minced or pressed. Cook over medium-high heat, stirring, until mixture boils and thickens. Remove from heat and stir in 2 tablespoons firmly packed **brown sugar,** 1½ tablespoons **lemon juice,** 1 tablespoon **soy sauce,** and ¼ to ½ teaspoon **crushed red pepper.** Let cool to room temperature before serving.

If made ahead, cover and refrigerate until next day; to reheat, cook over medium-low heat, stirring, until slightly warm. Thin with water, if necessary, to make a medium-thick sauce.

Poultry Roasting Time & Temperature Chart

What's the best way to roast poultry? How long will it take? How do I know when the bird is done? If you're unsure of the answers to these questions, you'll find the following guidelines helpful.

Preparing & roasting the bird. Remove neck and giblets from body cavity; rinse bird inside and out, then pat dry. Stuff chicken, game hens, or turkey, if you wish; then truss. (See pages 64 and 65 for stuffing recipes and techniques.) If you're roasting goose or duck, prick skin all over to allow fat to escape during cooking.

Estimate total cooking time by multiplying the bird's weight by the minutes per pound indicated below. If the bird is stuffed, add a few minutes to the total. Place bird, breast down, on a rack in a shallow roasting pan; rub skin generously with butter or margarine (or follow recipe directions). About halfway through estimated cooking time, turn bird breast up. Large turkeys can be awkward to turn by yourself, so enlist some help. Protecting hands, firmly hold turkey legs and neck end; turn.

Checking doneness. For a whole chicken or turkey, insert a meat thermometer in thickest part of thigh (not touching bone) after turning bird breast up. (For a turkey breast, insert in thickest part, not touching bone.) Begin checking thermometer three-quarters of the way through cooking; when it registers the correct temperature (see below), the bird is done.

Geese and ducks are fairly bony, so it's hard to insert a thermometer in the thigh without hitting bone. Game hens are too small for a thermometer to work correctly. To check doneness of these birds, slash meat near thighbone; it should no longer look pink.

If the bird finishes browning before it's completely cooked, cover it loosely with foil.

After taking the bird from the oven let it stand, loosely covered, for 10 to 20 minutes so the juices will settle back into the meat. Then carve (see page 94 for techniques).

Bird	Approximate weight (lbs.)	Approximate cooking time (minutes per lb.)	Oven temperature (°F)	Meat thermometer reading (°F)
Frying chicken	3–4	17–20	375°	185°
Roasting chicken	5–6	20–25	350°	185°
Rock Cornish game hen	1–1½	30–45	425°	—
Duckling	4–5	20–25	375°	—
Goose	8–14	10–12*	400°/325°*	—
Hen turkey	8–15	15	325°	185°
Tom turkey	16–30	12	325°	185°
Turkey breast Half, bone in Half, boneless	 2–4 2–4	 15–20 20–25	 350° 350°	 170° 170°
Turkey thigh	½–1½	60	350°	185°

*Roast goose at 400° for 1 hour, then reduce heat to 325°. Continue roasting for an additional 10 to 12 minutes per pound.

14 A **golden duo** of chicken thighs makes appealing fare, especially when accompanied by pasta with spinach and cheese. Diners add the finishing touch—a squeeze of orange—to Oven Chicken & Linguine (facing page).

Chicken Breasts with Spinach & Ham Filling

When a special occasion calls for a special dish, this entrée may be just what you're looking for.

    4 whole chicken breasts (about 1 lb.
       each), skinned, boned, and split (see
       page 93)
       Spinach & Ham Filling (recipe follows)
    2 tablespoons butter or margarine
    ½ cup chopped green onions (including
       tops)
    2 cloves garlic, minced or pressed
    ½ teaspoon dry mustard
    ¼ teaspoon dry rosemary
  1¾ cups regular-strength chicken broth,
       homemade (page 53) or purchased
       (one 14½-oz. can)
    ½ cup dry sherry
    ¼ cup chopped parsley
    ¾ cup whipping cream
       Pepper

Rinse chicken and pat dry. Place pieces one at a time, skinned side down, between 2 sheets of plastic wrap and pound with a flat-surfaced mallet until about ⅛ inch thick.

Prepare filling. Arrange pounded chicken pieces skinned side down; top each with about ⅛ of the filling. Spread filling almost to edges of each chicken piece, then roll up meat from narrow end. Place rolls, seam side down, in a 9 by 13-inch baking dish. (At this point, you may cover and refrigerate until next day. Let stand at room temperature for 1 hour before continuing.)

Melt butter in a wide frying pan over medium heat; add onions and garlic and cook, stirring, until soft. Stir in mustard, rosemary, broth, and sherry. Bring to a boil, then pour over chicken rolls. Cover dish with foil and bake in a 350° oven until chicken is no longer pink when slashed (40 to 45 minutes).

Drain pan juices into a wide frying pan; keep chicken rolls warm. Boil juices over high heat until reduced to 1½ cups. Add parsley and cream; boil until reduced to 1½ cups. Season to taste with pepper. Place one chicken roll on each of 8 dinner plates; spoon sauce over each. Makes 8 servings.

Spinach & Ham Filling. Discard tough stems from 1½ pounds **spinach;** rinse leaves well. Place leaves (with water that clings to them) in a 5 to 6-quart pan; cook over medium heat just until wilted (about 3 minutes). Drain; chop finely. Set aside.

Melt 2 tablespoons **butter** or margarine in a wide frying pan over medium-high heat. Add

⅔ cup thinly sliced **green onions** (including tops) and ½ pound **mushrooms,** thinly sliced. Cook, stirring, until vegetables are soft (about 10 minutes). Add spinach, 1 clove **garlic** (minced or pressed), 1 teaspoon **dry basil,** and 2 cups (8 to 10 oz.) chopped **cooked ham.** Cook, stirring, until almost all juices have evaporated (about 5 minutes). Season to taste with **pepper.** Remove from heat and let cool; then stir in 1 **egg,** lightly beaten.

Oven Chicken & Linguine

(Pictured on facing page)

For this whole-meal dish, you bake chicken, then toss linguine and spinach in the pan drippings.

    ½ cup (¼ lb.) butter or margarine
    1 medium-size onion, thinly sliced
    2 cloves garlic, minced or pressed
    1 tablespoon dry basil
    ½ teaspoon crushed red pepper
    8 chicken thighs (about 2½ lbs. *total*),
       rinsed and patted dry
    2 packages (10 oz. *each*) frozen chopped
       spinach
    8 ounces linguine or spaghetti
       Boiling salted water
    1 cup (about 5 oz.) grated Parmesan cheese
       Salt
    1 small orange (unpeeled), quartered

Melt butter in a 10 by 15-inch rimmed baking pan in a 400° oven; then remove pan from oven. Stir onion, garlic, basil, and pepper into butter. Place chicken, skin side down, in butter mixture; then turn over. Bake, uncovered, until meat near bone is no longer pink when slashed (about 45 minutes).

While chicken bakes, thaw spinach: place it in a 2 to 3-quart baking dish, cover, and set in oven for about 30 minutes. (After about 15 minutes, break into chunks with a fork to speed thawing.) Pour thawed spinach into a colander; squeeze out liquid.

Ten minutes before chicken is done, cook linguine in a large quantity of boiling salted water until *al dente* (about 13 minutes). Drain.

When chicken is done, lift from pan and keep warm. Add spinach to pan and stir to scrape browned bits free. Then add pasta and cheese; lift with 2 forks to mix well. Season to taste with salt.

Mound a portion of the pasta mixture on each of 4 dinner plates; flank with 2 pieces of chicken and an orange wedge. Before eating, squeeze orange over chicken and pasta. Makes 4 servings.

South-of-the-Border Baked Chicken

Green chile salsa and a chili-cumin crumb mixture coat these oven-fried chicken breasts. Served on a bed of lettuce and topped with sour cream, green onions, tomato, and avocado, they'll remind you of tostadas. Offer crisp tortilla chips alongside.

    3 whole chicken breasts (about 1 lb. *each*), skinned, boned, and split (see page 93)
    4 eggs
       Purchased green chile salsa or taco sauce
    2 cups fine dry bread crumbs
    2 teaspoons *each* chili powder and ground cumin
    1 teaspoon garlic salt
    ½ teaspoon ground oregano
    ¼ cup butter or margarine
    1 ripe avocado
    4 to 6 cups shredded iceberg lettuce
       About 1 cup sour cream or plain yogurt
       About 6 tablespoons thinly sliced green onions (including tops)
    12 to 18 cherry tomatoes
    1 or 2 limes, cut into wedges

Rinse chicken and pat dry. Set aside.

In a shallow bowl, beat together eggs and 4 to 5 tablespoons salsa. In another shallow bowl, combine bread crumbs, chili powder, cumin, garlic salt, and oregano. Dip one chicken piece in egg mixture to coat; drain briefly, then dip in crumb mixture to coat. Shake off excess crumbs. Repeat with remaining chicken pieces.

Melt butter in a 10 by 15-inch rimmed baking pan in a 375° oven. Add chicken; turn to coat with butter. Bake, uncovered, until meat is no longer pink when slashed in thickest part (30 to 35 minutes).

Pit, peel, and slice avocado. Line each of 6 dinner plates with lettuce; top with one piece of chicken. Garnish with a dollop of sour cream, avocado, onions, tomatoes, and lime wedges. Pass additional sour cream and salsa at the table. Makes 6 servings.

Honey Citrus Chicken

Honey, fruit juices, and sweet spices make a fresh-tasting baste for this easy-on-the-cook dish.

       3½ to 4-pound frying chicken, cut up
    ⅓ cup honey
    2 teaspoons *each* grated lemon peel and orange peel
    ¼ cup fresh lemon juice
    1½ teaspoons Dijon mustard
    ½ teaspoon curry powder
    ½ teaspoon ground ginger or 1 teaspoon minced fresh ginger
    1 large orange (unpeeled), ends trimmed

Reserve chicken neck and giblets for other uses, if desired. Rinse chicken and pat dry; then place, skin side down, in a 10 by 15-inch rimmed baking pan. In a small bowl, stir together honey, lemon peel, orange peel, lemon juice, mustard, curry powder, and ginger. Brush half the mixture over chicken pieces. Bake, uncovered, in a 375° oven for 30 minutes, basting occasionally with pan juices. Then turn chicken over and brush with remaining honey mixture. Continue to bake, basting occasionally, until chicken is browned and meat near thighbone is no longer pink when slashed (about 30 more minutes).

Transfer chicken to a platter. Cut orange in half lengthwise; then cut crosswise into ¼-inch slices. Tuck orange slices around chicken. Spoon pan juices over all. Makes 4 or 5 servings.

Fila Chicken Packets

Flaky and buttery outside, moist inside, fila rolls make a striking company dish. To keep fila from drying out as you work with it, keep sheets covered with plastic wrap or a barely damp towel until needed.

    3 whole chicken breasts (about 1 lb. *each*) skinned, boned, and split (see page 93)
    ¾ cup *each* chopped green onions (including tops) and mayonnaise
    3 tablespoons lemon juice
    ¾ teaspoon dry tarragon
    3 cloves garlic, minced or pressed
    ⅔ cup butter or margarine, melted
    12 sheets fila (thawed if frozen)
       Salt and pepper
    2 tablespoons grated Parmesan cheese

Rinse chicken and pat dry. Set aside.

In a small bowl, stir together onions, mayonnaise, lemon juice, tarragon, and 2 cloves of the garlic; set aside. Combine remaining 1 clove garlic with butter.

To make each packet, place one sheet of fila on a flat surface and brush it with about 2 teaspoons of the garlic butter; arrange a second sheet on top and brush it with 2 more teaspoons garlic butter. Lightly sprinkle all sides of one chicken piece with salt and pepper, then spread one side with about 1½ tablespoons of the mayonnaise mixture. Place chicken, mayonnaise side down, in center of fila about 2 inches up from one end. Spread chicken with 1½ more tablespoons mayonnaise mixture. Flip end of fila over chicken and roll once; then fold both long sides over chicken and roll up completely.

Brush packets with remaining garlic butter and sprinkle with cheese. (At this point, you may arrange packets, in a single layer, in a container with a tight-fitting lid and freeze for up to 1 month. Thaw completely, covered, before baking.)

To bake, arrange fila packets, seam side down and slightly apart, in an ungreased 10 by 15-inch rimmed baking pan. Bake, uncovered, in a 375° oven until golden brown (20 to 25 minutes). Makes 6 servings.

Crispy Oven-fried Chicken for a Dozen

When warm, sunny days bring thoughts of picnicking, chicken is often a favorite choice. This recipe serves a hungry dozen, and it's just as good cold as it is hot. Line baking pans with foil for easy cleanup.

- 3 frying chickens (3 to 3½ lbs. *each*), cut up
- ¾ cup (¼ lb. plus ¼ cup) butter or margarine
- 1¾ cups all-purpose flour
- ⅔ cup yellow cornmeal
- 1 tablespoon chili powder
- 2 teaspoons seasoned salt
- 1¼ teaspoons *each* thyme and oregano leaves
- ½ cup grated Parmesan cheese
- 1½ cups buttermilk

Reserve chicken necks and giblets for other uses, if desired. Rinse chicken and pat dry; set aside.

Line two 10 by 15-inch rimmed baking pans with foil. Place half the butter in each pan; set pans in a 400° oven until butter is melted.

Meanwhile, place flour, cornmeal, chili powder, seasoned salt, thyme, oregano, and cheese in a bag; stir with a spoon to mix. Pour buttermilk into a bowl. Dip a few chicken pieces in buttermilk and drain briefly; place in bag and shake to coat with flour mixture. Repeat with remaining chicken pieces.

Place half the chicken pieces in each pan; turn to coat with butter, then arrange skin side down. Bake, uncovered, for 25 minutes. Turn pieces over, switch position of pans in oven, and continue to bake until meat near thighbone is no longer pink when slashed (25 to 30 more minutes). Makes about 12 servings.

Coconut Curried Chicken Winglets

The ingredients may sound unusual, but the results are unquestionably delicious: moist, coconut-flavored meat with a crunchy, curry-seasoned coating. Serve these winglets for an informal main dish or appetizer (be sure to provide plenty of napkins).

- 4½ pounds chicken wings (about 24), rinsed and patted dry
- 1 cup milk
- ½ teaspoon coconut extract
- 2 cups instant mashed potato mix
- 4 teaspoons curry powder
- 3 tablespoons sweetened flaked coconut
- 6 tablespoons butter or margarine, melted
- 2 cloves garlic, minced or pressed

Cut chicken wings apart at both joints; reserve tips for other uses, if desired. In a large bowl, combine milk and coconut extract; add winglets and stir well. Cover and refrigerate for at least 2 hours or until next day.

In a medium-size bowl, combine potato mix, curry powder, and coconut. Stir chicken to moisten; then lift out one winglet, drain briefly, and roll in potato mixture to coat completely. Repeat with remaining winglets. Place winglets slightly apart on 2 well-greased 10 by 15-inch rimmed baking pans and one well-greased 7 by 11-inch baking pan.

Combine butter and garlic; drizzle over chicken. Bake, uncovered, in a 375° oven until well browned and crisp (about 45 minutes), switching position of pans in oven halfway through baking. Serve hot. Makes 10 to 12 appetizer servings or 5 or 6 main-dish servings.

Easy Baked Chicken Kiev

Though boning and pounding chicken breasts for this dish does take some time, the results are impressive. You can assemble the bundles a day in advance, then pop them into the oven just before guests arrive.

   4 **whole chicken breasts** (about 1 lb. *each*) skinned, boned, and split (see page 93)
  ½ **cup** *each* **fine dry bread crumbs** and grated **Parmesan cheese**
  1½ **teaspoons oregano leaves**
  ½ **teaspoon garlic salt**
  ¼ **teaspoon pepper**
  ¼ **cup butter** or **margarine**, softened
   1 **tablespoon chopped parsley**
   4 **ounces jack cheese,** cut into 8 strips (*each* ½ inch thick and 1½ inches long)
   6 **tablespoons butter** or **margarine,** melted

Rinse chicken and pat dry. Place pieces one at a time, skinned side down, between 2 sheets of plastic wrap and pound with a flat-surfaced mallet until about ⅛ inch thick.

In a shallow bowl, combine bread crumbs, Parmesan cheese, 1 teaspoon of the oregano, garlic salt, and pepper; set aside. In a small bowl, stir together the ¼ cup butter, remaining ½ teaspoon oregano, and parsley.

Arrange pounded chicken pieces skinned side down. Spread about ½ tablespoon of the butter mixture across each piece about an inch from one long side; place a strip of jack cheese over butter mixture. Fold short ends over filling, then fold in long side and roll to enclose filling.

Dip each bundle in the 6 tablespoons melted butter and drain briefly; then roll in crumb mixture until evenly coated. Place bundles, seam side down and slightly apart, in a 10 by 15-inch rimmed baking pan. Drizzle with any remaining butter. Cover and refrigerate for at least 4 hours or until next day.

Bake, uncovered, in a 425° oven until chicken is no longer pink when lightly slashed (don't cut through to filling)—about 20 minutes. Serve at once. Makes 8 servings.

Mexican-style Chicken Kiev

Follow directions for **Easy Baked Chicken Kiev,** but omit oregano. Instead, use a mixture of 1 teaspoon **chili powder** and ½ teaspoon **ground cumin.** Remove chiles from 1 large can (7 oz.) **whole green chiles;** discard pith and seeds. Cut chiles lengthwise into 1-inch strips; divide into 8 equal portions. When filling each chicken breast, arrange one portion of chiles atop each strip of cheese.

Serve baked chicken with the following tomato sauce: In a small pan, stir together 1 can (15 oz.) **tomato sauce,** ½ teaspoon *each* **ground cumin** and **sugar,** and ⅓ cup sliced **green onions** (including tops). Cook over medium heat, stirring, until hot. Season sauce to taste with **salt, pepper,** and **liquid hot pepper seasoning.**

Pomegranate Chicken

(Pictured on facing page)

Ruby red pomegranate juice lends tang to chicken, first in a marinade, then in an unusual cream sauce. Squeeze the juice from fresh pomegranate halves, using a lemon reamer; or, if the fresh fruit isn't available, use unsweetened pomegranate juice purchased from a health food store or well-stocked supermarket.

To soak up all the sauce, serve the chicken atop a bed of rice.

   1 **cup unsweetened pomegranate juice** (from about 5 large pomegranates)
   3 **tablespoons soy sauce**
  ½ **teaspoon** *each* **dry rosemary** and grated **fresh ginger**
   2 **large cloves garlic,** minced or pressed
   6 **whole chicken legs, thighs attached** (about 3 lbs. *total*), skinned
  ½ **cup whipping cream**
  ⅓ **cup pomegranate seeds** (optional)
      Fresh rosemary or **parsley sprigs**

In a 9 by 13-inch baking dish, stir together pomegranate juice, soy, dry rosemary, ginger, and garlic; set aside. Rinse chicken, pat dry, and place in dish; turn to coat with marinade. Cover and refrigerate for 8 hours, turning chicken pieces several times.

Drain off and reserve marinade; then arrange chicken pieces slightly apart in dish. Bake, uncovered, in a 350° oven until meat near thighbone is no longer pink when slashed (about 45 minutes), basting occasionally with reserved marinade.

Transfer chicken to a platter and keep warm. Skim and discard fat from pan drippings, then pour drippings into a 1½ to 2-quart pan; stir in cream. Bring to a boil over high heat and boil rapidly until sauce is slightly thickened and reduced to about ¾ cup. Spoon sauce evenly over chicken; garnish with pomegranate seeds (if desired) and rosemary sprigs. Makes 6 servings.

Jewel-like pomegranate seeds adorn a wheel of succulent baked chicken legs. To soak up every drop of the piquant, creamy sauce, serve Pomegranate Chicken (facing page) on a bed of fluffy rice.

19

Skillet Specialties

Chicken pan-fried, stir-fried & deep-fried

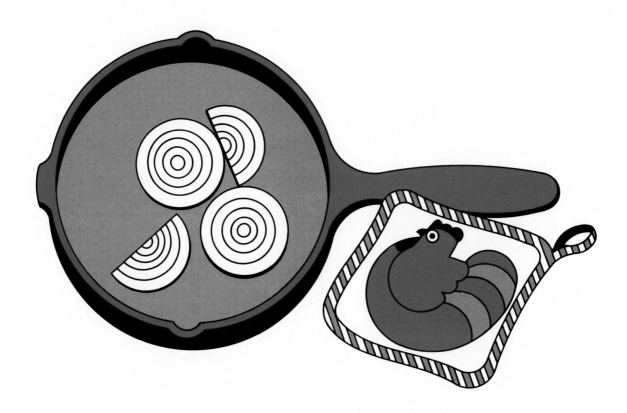

Here's proof that there's more than one way to fry a chicken! Three different techniques—pan-frying, stir-frying, and deep-frying—produce three different kinds of range-top dishes.

Traditional fried chicken is probably the most popular kind of pan-fried chicken, perfect for family dinners and picnics. Other pan-fried entrées are suited to more elegant occasions—boned breasts in a creamy chutney-wine sauce, for example.

Stir-fried chicken is a top choice for a wholesome meal made in short order. Rapid cooking over high heat seals the juices into boneless morsels of light or dark meat. You'll find traditional Chinese stir-fries as well as a few less conventional dishes, such as an Italian-style sandwich filling for pocket bread and a "tropical" stir-fry with lime and papaya. For any stir-fry, heat the pan first; then add food and stir constantly with a light, lifting motion to ensure even cooking.

When you want meat with an extra-crisp coating, choose deep-fried chicken. Hot oil quickly cooks meat to a crunch on the outside, locking flavor inside. Try Chinese chicken salad or Japanese tempura; or make crisp chicken nuggets to serve with dipping sauces. (To ensure even cooking, check oil temperature often with a deep-frying thermometer.)

20

Chicken in Orange Cream

Oranges add a delicate citrus flavor to the sour cream sauce that coats these pan-fried chicken thighs. Since the sauce is so rich, keep accompaniments simple—asparagus spears or green beans, for example.

         8 chicken thighs (about 2½ lbs. *total*)
            Salt and pepper
            All-purpose flour
        ¼ cup butter or margarine
        ¼ cup salad oil
         1 clove garlic, minced or pressed
       1½ tablespoons *each* thinly sliced
            green onion (including top) and
            orange juice
         1 teaspoon grated orange peel
        ½ cup dry white wine
         2 teaspoons sugar
        ¼ teaspoon dry tarragon
        ½ cup sour cream
            Orange wedges

Rinse chicken and pat dry. Sprinkle on all sides with salt and pepper; dredge in flour and shake off excess.

In each of 2 wide frying pans over medium heat, melt half the butter in half the oil. Place 4 thighs in each pan; cook, turning, until well browned on all sides and meat near bone is no longer pink when slashed—about 20 minutes. (Or cook thighs, 4 at a time, in one pan, using a total of 2 tablespoons *each* butter and oil.) Transfer to a platter and keep warm.

Make sauce in one pan. Pour off and discard drippings, leaving browned bits in bottom of pan. Add garlic, onion, orange juice, orange peel, wine, and any juices that have drained from chicken. Increase heat to medium-high. Bring to a boil, stirring to scrape browned bits free; remove from heat. Stir sugar, tarragon, and 1½ teaspoons flour into sour cream; then stir sour cream into wine mixture. Return to heat and cook, stirring, until sauce comes to a gentle boil. Season to taste with salt and pepper; pour over chicken. Pass orange wedges to squeeze over individual portions. Makes 4 servings.

Chicken in Lemon Cream

Follow directions for **Chicken in Orange Cream,** but omit garlic. Substitute **lemon juice** for orange juice and **thyme leaves** for tarragon. Instead of orange peel, use ½ teaspoon **lemon peel.** Use **lemon wedges** in place of orange wedges.

Chicken Livers on Crisp Potato Pancake

Chicken livers in a creamy mustard sauce, spooned over a giant-size crisp potato pancake, are a treat indeed. Pair this dish with a red table wine and a tossed green salad for an excellent informal supper menu.

        ½ pound chicken livers
         4 slices bacon
         1 pound russet potatoes
         1 tablespoon all-purpose flour
         4 tablespoons butter or margarine
         2 teaspoons Dijon mustard
        ¼ cup whipping cream
        ¼ cup finely chopped parsley
            Salt and pepper
            Lemon wedges

Rinse livers and pat dry. Cut each liver in half, then set livers aside.

In a wide frying pan with a nonstick finish, cook bacon over medium heat until crisp; then lift out, drain, crumble, and set aside. Pour off and reserve drippings.

Peel potatoes; coarsely shred into a bowl of cold water, stir, and drain well. Mix flour into drained potatoes.

Melt 1 tablespoon of the butter in pan over medium heat. Add potatoes and pat into an even layer. Cover and cook for 5 minutes. Uncover and cook, pressing to compact into a solid layer, until bottom is browned. Slide potato cake onto a flat plate or rimless baking sheet. Melt 1 more tablespoon butter in pan; invert cake back into pan. Cook until browned on bottom, then slide onto a serving plate and keep warm.

Add ½ tablespoon of the reserved bacon drippings to pan. Add half the livers and cook, turning as needed, until browned on outside but still pink in center when slashed (about 1 minute); transfer to a plate. Repeat with remaining livers, adding ½ tablespoon more drippings to pan. Set livers aside.

Add 2 more tablespoons of the bacon drippings to pan with remaining 2 tablespoons butter, mustard, and cream. Increase heat to high; boil, stirring to scrape browned bits free, until large, shiny bubbles form. Add livers (and any juices that have drained from them) and parsley; stir just until heated through. Season to taste with salt and pepper.

Spoon liver mixture over pancake, top with bacon, and garnish with lemon wedges. Cut into wedges to serve. Makes 3 or 4 servings.

22 **T**ender breast meat envelops a savory spinach-bacon filling for an elegant
entrée. Accompany Spinach-stuffed Chicken Breasts (facing page)
with steamed asparagus and cheese-topped scalloped potatoes.

Spinach-stuffed Chicken Breasts

(Pictured on facing page)

When carefully slit in the thickest part, chicken breasts make neat "pockets" for a spinach stuffing.

- 8 slices bacon
- 1 large onion, finely chopped
- 1 package (10 oz.) frozen chopped spinach, thawed and squeezed dry
- 1 egg, lightly beaten
- ½ cup seasoned croutons, coarsely crushed
- ½ teaspoon garlic salt
- 4 whole chicken breasts (about 1 lb. *each*), skinned, boned, and split (see page 93)
- 3 tablespoons salad oil

In a wide frying pan, cook bacon over medium heat until crisp; then lift out, drain, crumble, and set aside. Discard all but 2 tablespoons drippings.

Add onion to pan and cook, stirring, until soft; remove pan from heat, then stir in spinach, egg, croutons, garlic salt, and bacon.

Rinse chicken and pat dry. With a sharp knife, cut a deep pocket in thick side of each breast half to within about 1 inch of short ends and other long side. Stuff each breast half with ⅛ of the spinach mixture, then fasten closed with wooden picks.

Wipe frying pan clean. Add oil and heat over medium heat. Add chicken, a portion at a time; cook, turning after 6 to 7 minutes, until meat is no longer pink when slashed (12 to 15 minutes *total*). Makes 8 servings.

Golden Chicken Cutlets

Serve crisp, herb-seasoned chicken cutlets hot or cold, for a picnic or summer buffet.

- 3 whole chicken breasts (about 1 lb. *each*), skinned, boned, and split (see page 93)
- ¼ cup all-purpose flour
- ½ teaspoon salt
- ⅛ teaspoon *each* white pepper, ground nutmeg, and marjoram leaves
- 1 egg
- 1 tablespoon water
- ½ cup fine dry bread crumbs
- ⅓ cup grated Parmesan cheese
- ¼ cup butter or margarine
- 2 tablespoons olive oil or salad oil
- ½ cup dry white wine
  Lemon wedges

Rinse chicken and pat dry. Place pieces one at a time, skinned side down, between 2 sheets of plastic wrap and pound with a flat-surfaced mallet until about ¼ inch thick.

In a dish, mix flour, salt, pepper, nutmeg, and marjoram. Beat egg and water in a second dish; mix bread crumbs and cheese in a third. Coat chicken with flour mixture, then egg, then crumb mixture.

Melt butter in oil in a wide frying pan over medium-high heat. Add chicken, a portion at a time; cook, turning after 2 to 3 minutes, until no longer pink when slashed (4 to 6 minutes *total*). Transfer to a platter and keep warm.

Add wine to pan; boil over high heat until slightly reduced, stirring to scrape browned bits free. Pour over chicken. Pass lemon wedges to squeeze over meat. Makes 6 servings.

Chicken Breasts with Chutney & Madeira

Chutney and Madeira team up with cream and ginger to make a melt-in-the-mouth sauce for chicken.

- 3 whole chicken breasts (about 1 lb. *each*), skinned, boned, and split (see page 93)
- 2 tablespoons butter or margarine
- 2 green onions (including tops), sliced
- ½ teaspoon minced fresh ginger
- 3 tablespoons chopped Major Grey's chutney
- ⅓ cup Madeira
- ¾ cup regular-strength chicken broth, homemade (page 53) or purchased
- ¾ cup whipping cream
  Salt and pepper
- 2 tablespoons chopped crystallized ginger
  Parsley sprigs

Rinse chicken and pat dry. Melt butter in a wide frying pan over medium heat. Add chicken, a portion at a time, without crowding; cook, turning after 5 minutes, until no longer pink when slashed in thickest part (about 10 minutes *total*). As chicken is cooked, transfer to a platter and keep warm.

Add onions, fresh ginger, chutney, Madeira, and broth to pan. Increase heat to high and boil, stirring, until reduced by half (about 4 minutes). Add cream and any juices that have drained from chicken; boil briefly. Season to taste with salt and pepper. Spoon half the sauce over chicken; sprinkle with crystallized ginger and garnish with parsley. Pass remaining sauce at the table. Makes 6 servings.

An Appetizer Showcase

Versatile and flavorful, chicken has long been a favorite choice for appetizers. Our sampler includes a tasty array of recipes featuring different parts of the bird: tidbits of breast meat wrapped in fresh spinach leaves, livers made into pâté and rumaki, crisp deep-fried wings, and an herb-seasoned spread made with dark meat. For more hors d'oeuvre suggestions, look under "Appetizers" in the index.

Chicken Liver Pâté

Creamy pâté is classic, as appropriate at a formal dinner party as at a country picnic.

- ½ pound chicken livers
- 1 large onion, thinly sliced
- 1¾ cups regular-strength chicken broth, homemade (page 53) or purchased (one 14½-oz. can)
- ½ cup (¼ lb.) butter or margarine, cut into chunks and softened
- 2 teaspoons brandy (optional)
- 2 tablespoons chopped parsley
- ¼ teaspoon pepper
- 1 teaspoon thyme leaves
  Salt
  Crackers or toast triangles

Rinse livers and pat dry. Combine livers, onion, and broth in a 1 to 2-quart pan. Bring to a boil over high heat; reduce heat, cover, and simmer for 10 minutes.

Remove from heat and let stand, covered, for 10 minutes; then drain (reserve broth for other uses, if desired).

In a blender or food processor, whirl livers and onion until smooth. Add butter; whirl until well blended. Add brandy (if used), parsley, pepper, and thyme; whirl until very smooth. Season to taste with salt. Spoon into a small container, cover, and refrigerate for at least 24 hours or up to 1 week. Serve with crackers or toast triangles. Makes 1¾ cups.

Chicken Rillettes

Once considered peasant fare, French *rillettes* (hearty meat spreads) are often featured today in stylish delicatessens and restaurants. Offer our chicken version as a topping for tiny open-faced sandwiches.

- 3½ pounds (about 7) whole chicken legs, thighs attached
- 1 teaspoon *each* salt and pepper
- 1 clove garlic, minced or pressed
- ½ teaspoon *each* thyme leaves and dry rosemary
- 1 bay leaf
- ¼ cup finely chopped shallots or green onions (including tops)
- ⅓ cup *each* dry white wine and water (or use ⅔ cup water)
- ½ cup (¼ lb.) unsalted butter or margarine, softened

Rinse chicken, pat dry, and cut apart at joints. Place meat in a 4 to 5-quart casserole or oven-proof pan and add salt, pepper, garlic, thyme, rosemary, bay leaf, shallots, wine, and water. Cover tightly and bake in a 250° oven until meat is so tender it falls apart when prodded with a fork (about 4 hours).

Pour chicken mixture through a colander, reserving juices. Let cool; discard bay leaf, bones, skin, and tendons. Finely shred meat. Skim and discard fat from juices.

With a heavy spoon or your hands, work together meat, juices, and butter until well blended. Pack into a bowl, crock, or terrine (about 5-cup size). If made ahead, cover and refrigerate for up to 1 week; serve at room temperature. Makes 5 cups.

Rumaki

These bacon-wrapped chicken liver treats have been cocktail-party favorites for years.

¾ **pound chicken livers**
½ **pound sliced bacon**
1 **can (8 oz.) whole water chestnuts,
    drained**
½ **cup soy sauce**
1 **small clove garlic, minced or pressed**
1 **small dried hot red chile, crushed**
6 **thin slices fresh ginger**

Rinse livers and pat dry; then cut in half. Cut bacon slices in half crosswise. Hold a piece of liver and a water chestnut together; wrap with a piece of bacon and fasten with a wooden pick.

In a bowl, stir together soy, garlic, chile, and ginger. Add chicken liver bundles; cover and refrigerate, turning occasionally, for at least 3 hours or until next day.

Lift rumaki from marinade, drain, and place on a rack in a broiler pan. Broil 6 inches below heat, turning once, until bacon is crisp (about 7 minutes *total*). Makes about 1½ dozen.

Chicken Wings with Garlic Sauce

Crisp fried chicken wings with a sweet-sour garlic sauce are a traditional Thai appetizer.

   Garlic Sauce (recipe follows)
12 **chicken wings (about 2¼ lbs. *total*)**
   Salad oil
2 **eggs**
   All-purpose flour

Prepare Garlic Sauce; set aside. Rinse chicken and pat very dry. Cut wings apart at joints; reserve wingtips for other uses, if desired. In a deep, heavy pan, heat 1½ inches of oil to 350°F on a deep-frying thermometer. In a shallow pan, beat eggs; dip wings in beaten egg, then in flour to coat lightly. Lower chicken into oil, 4 to 6 pieces at a time, and cook, turning, until meat near bone is no longer pink when slashed (5 to 7 minutes). Lift out and drain on paper towels. Arrange on an ovenproof tray and keep warm in a 200° oven until all chicken has been cooked. Serve with sauce for dipping. Makes 2 dozen.

Garlic Sauce. In a 1 to 2-quart pan, stir together ½ cup **sugar**, ¼ cup **water**, ⅓ cup **distilled white vinegar**, ¼ teaspoon **salt**, and 15 cloves **garlic**, minced or pressed. Cover and cook over

medium-low heat until garlic is translucent (about 10 minutes). Mix 1½ teaspoons **cornstarch** with 2 teaspoons **water**. Stir into garlic mixture; cook, stirring, until mixture boils.

In a blender or food processor, combine garlic mixture, 8 more cloves **garlic,** and 1 small **fresh hot chile,** cut up; whirl until puréed.

Spinach-wrapped Chicken with Curry Mayonnaise

Soy-seasoned chicken chunks wrapped in spinach make tidy "packages" for dipping.

2 **whole chicken breasts (about 1 lb.
    each), split**
1¾ **cups regular-strength chicken broth,
    homemade (page 53) or purchased
    (one 14½-oz. can)**
¼ **cup soy sauce**
1 **tablespoon Worcestershire**
   Curry Mayonnaise (recipe follows)
   About 1 pound spinach, rinsed well
8 **cups boiling water**

Rinse chicken, pat dry, and place in a wide frying pan; then add broth, soy, and Worcestershire. Bring to a boil over medium heat; reduce heat, cover, and simmer until chicken is no longer pink when slashed in thickest part (15 to 20 minutes). Meanwhile, prepare Curry Mayonnaise.

Lift chicken from broth; let cool. Discard skin and bones; cut meat into 1-inch chunks. Reserve broth for other uses, if desired.

Discard spinach stems, keeping leaves whole; place leaves in a colander. Pour boiling water over leaves. Drain thoroughly; let cool.

To assemble each bundle, place one chunk of chicken at stem end of a spinach leaf. Roll over once, fold leaf in on both sides, and roll up completely. Secure end of leaf with a wooden pick. Cover and refrigerate for at least 1 hour or until next day. Serve with Curry Mayonnaise for dipping. Makes 4 to 5 dozen appetizers.

Curry Mayonnaise. In a bowl, combine ¼ cup *each* **mayonnaise** and **sour cream,** 2 teaspoons **curry powder,** 2 tablespoons chopped **Major Grey's chutney,** and 1 teaspoon grated **orange peel.** Cover; refrigerate for at least 1 hour.

Southern Fried Chicken

(Pictured on facing page)

There's a trick to the crisp crust on this golden fried chicken: you refrigerate the floured pieces for an hour, then flour them again just before frying. The chicken is marvelous as is, but for a real feast, serve it with our milk gravy.

If you remove the browned bits from the cooking oil, you can recycle it to fry chicken another time. Let the oil cool, then pour it through a strainer lined with several thicknesses of cheese-cloth into a jar. Refrigerate the oil until needed; discard it when it darkens or starts to smell rancid.

> 3 to 3½-pound frying chicken, cut up
> 1 egg
> All-purpose flour
> Solid vegetable shortening
> Milk Gravy (optional; recipe follows)

Reserve chicken neck and giblets for other uses, if desired. Rinse chicken and pat dry; set aside.

In a shallow bowl, lightly beat egg. Place about ½ cup flour in another shallow bowl. Dip chicken pieces, one at a time, in egg until evenly moistened; then roll in flour and shake off excess. Place pieces slightly apart on a baking sheet and refrigerate, uncovered, for 1 hour.

In a heavy 12 to 14-inch frying pan over medium heat, melt enough shortening to reach a depth of ¼ inch. Meanwhile, recoat chicken with flour; shake off excess. To test temperature of fat, drop a pinch of flour into pan; flour should float and sizzle on hot fat. If flour sinks to bottom of pan and disperses, fat is not hot enough.

Arrange chicken pieces skin side down in a single layer, without crowding, in hot fat. (Arrange legs and thighs in center of pan where heat is concentrated, since dark meat pieces take longer to cook.) Allow enough space between pieces for fat to bubble and sizzle; this assures even cooking and browning.

Cook chicken for 15 minutes. Turn pieces over with tongs and continue to cook until meat near thighbone is no longer pink when slashed (15 to 20 more minutes). Lift out chicken and drain on paper towels. Keep warm. Prepare gravy, if desired; pass at the table. Makes about 4 servings.

Milk Gravy. Pour off and reserve **pan drippings** from frying pan, leaving browned bits in pan. Return 5 tablespoons drippings to pan (discard remainder); stir to scrape browned bits free. Blend in ¼ cup **all-purpose flour** and cook over medium-high heat, stirring, until bubbly. Gradually pour in 2½ cups **milk** and continue to cook and stir until gravy boils and thickens. Season to taste with **salt** and **pepper**.

Easy Fried Chicken

Everyone loves fried chicken, but some cooks dislike the spattering that comes from cooking with a fair amount of oil. Spatters are minimized in this recipe, because you cover the pan for the first half of the cooking time.

If you take fried chicken on a picnic, be sure to package it properly to prevent spoilage. Chicken to be served hot should be packaged in foil when piping hot, then wrapped in insulating material such as newspapers. If chicken is to be served cold, refrigerate it until well chilled, then pack it in an insulated chest.

> 3 to 3½-pound frying chicken, cut up
> 2 tablespoons dry sherry
> ½ cup all-purpose flour
> ½ teaspoon *each* salt, garlic salt, and paprika
> ¼ teaspoon *each* pepper, rubbed sage, thyme leaves, and dry basil
> Salad oil

Reserve chicken neck and giblets for other uses, if desired. Rinse chicken, pat dry, place in a shallow pan, and sprinkle with sherry. Let stand for 10 minutes. Meanwhile, place flour, salt, garlic salt, paprika, pepper, sage, thyme, and basil in a bag; stir with a spoon to mix.

Into a heavy 12 to 14-inch frying pan with a lid, pour oil to a depth of ½ inch. Place chicken pieces (do not pat dry), a few at a time, in bag and shake to coat.

Arrange chicken pieces skin side down in a single layer, without crowding, in *unheated* oil. (Place legs and thighs in center of pan where heat is concentrated, since dark meat takes longer to cook.) Allow enough space between pieces for oil to bubble and sizzle; this assures even cooking and browning.

Cover pan and place over medium-high heat. Cook until chicken begins sizzling loudly (about 7 minutes); then continue to cook for 15 more minutes. Uncover pan; turn pieces over with tongs and continue to cook, uncovered, until meat near thighbone is no longer pink when slashed (about 10 more minutes). Lift out chicken and drain briefly on paper towels. Serve hot or cold. Makes about 4 servings.

This down-home feast has been an American favorite for generations: crusty Southern Fried Chicken (facing page), corn on the cob, and hot biscuits with honey.

Salsa Chicken with Cheese

Bright tomato-chile salsa and shredded Cheddar cheese dress up pan-fried chicken breasts. Accompany the dish with mugs of cold beer, a tossed green salad, and hot cooked rice or warm flour tortillas.

   3 whole chicken breasts (about 1 lb. *each*), skinned, boned, and split (see page 93)
1½ tablespoons butter or margarine
1½ tablespoons salad oil
   1 medium-size onion, chopped
   1 clove garlic, minced or pressed
   2 stalks celery, thinly sliced
   1 can (4 oz.) diced green chiles
   1 can (16 oz.) stewed tomatoes
   ½ cup regular-strength chicken broth, homemade (page 53) or purchased
   ¼ teaspoon ground cumin
   ½ teaspoon *each* oregano leaves and sugar
     Salt and pepper
1½ cups (6 oz.) shredded Cheddar cheese

Rinse chicken and pat dry. Place pieces one at a time, skinned side down, between 2 sheets of plastic wrap and pound with a flat-surfaced mallet until about ¼ inch thick.

Melt butter in oil in a wide frying pan over medium-high heat. Add chicken, a portion at a time, without crowding; cook, turning after 2 to 3 minutes, until golden on outside and no longer pink when slashed (4 to 6 minutes *total*). As chicken is cooked, transfer to an ovenproof platter and keep warm.

Add onion, garlic, and celery to pan; cook, stirring, until onion is soft. Add chiles, tomatoes and their liquid, broth, cumin, oregano, and sugar. Cook, uncovered, stirring frequently, until thickened (about 10 minutes). Add any juices that have drained from chicken, then season to taste with salt and pepper. Pour sauce over chicken. Sprinkle with cheese and broil 3 inches below heat until cheese is melted. Makes 6 servings.

Sautéed Chicken with Two-tone Pears

The colors of red and yellow pears contrast handsomely in this elegant entrée. (If red pears are unavailable, use two yellow ones.)

   3 whole chicken breasts (about 1 lb. *each*), skinned, boned, and split (see page 93)
     All-purpose flour
     About 3 tablespoons butter or margarine
   1 *each* small red and yellow pear
   1 cup dry white wine
   ¾ cup whipping cream
   ¾ cup regular-strength chicken broth, homemade (page 53) or purchased
   ½ teaspoon fresh rosemary leaves or ¼ teaspoon dry rosemary
   6 lemon wedges

Rinse chicken and pat dry. Place pieces one at a time, skinned side down, between 2 sheets of plastic wrap and pound with a flat-surfaced mallet until about ¼ inch thick.

Dust chicken with flour; shake off excess. Melt 1½ tablespoons of the butter in a wide frying pan over medium-high heat. Add chicken, a portion at a time, without crowding. Cook, turning once, until no longer pink when slashed (about 5 minutes *total*). As chicken is cooked, transfer to a platter and keep warm; add more butter to pan as needed.

Core pears and cut into ½-inch-thick wedges. Arrange in pan in a single layer; cook over medium-high heat just until warm (2 to 3 minutes), carefully turning once. Arrange over chicken; keep warm.

Add wine, cream, broth, and rosemary to pan. Bring to a boil, stirring to scrape browned bits free; boil, uncovered, until reduced by half (7 to 8 minutes). Add any juices that have drained from chicken; bring sauce to a boil and pour around chicken. Garnish with lemon wedges. Makes 6 servings.

Chicken Kung Pao Style

This version of Szechwan's *kung pao* is a bit milder than its fiery traditional counterpart.

   2 whole chicken breasts (about 1 lb. *each*), skinned, boned, and split (see page 93)
   2 tablespoons cornstarch
   3 tablespoons *each* soy sauce, water, and dry sherry
   2 tablespoons hoisin sauce
   1 teaspoon sesame oil
   3 tablespoons salad oil
   6 small dried hot red chiles
   2 cloves garlic, minced
   ¾ cup sliced green onions (including tops)
   1 can (8 oz.) water chestnuts, drained and sliced

Rinse chicken and pat dry; cut into ¾-inch chunks. In a bowl, stir together cornstarch, soy, water, and sherry. Add chicken and mix well; then cover and let stand for 1 hour.

Lift chicken from marinade and drain briefly (reserve marinade); set aside. Stir hoisin and sesame oil into marinade; set aside.

Place a wok or wide frying pan over high heat. When pan is hot, add salad oil. When oil begins to heat, add chicken and cook, stirring, until lightly browned (about 3 minutes). Lift out and set aside.

Add chiles to pan and cook, stirring, until black. Add garlic and all but 1 tablespoon of the onions; cook, stirring, for 15 seconds. Return chicken to pan with water chestnuts and marinade; cook, stirring, until sauce boils and thickens. Spoon chicken mixture into a serving dish and sprinkle with reserved onions. Makes about 3 servings.

Chicken Pocket Sandwiches

Boned, cubed chicken seasoned with garlic, anchovies, and olives makes a quick-to-cook sandwich filling. We suggest spooning the filling into pocket bread halves, but use crusty rolls if you prefer.

- 6 **tablespoons butter or margarine**
- 3 **cloves garlic, minced or pressed**
- 3 **pocket breads, halved crosswise**
- 2 **whole chicken breasts (about 1 lb. *each*), skinned, boned, and split (see page 93)**
- 1 **tablespoon olive oil or salad oil**
- ¼ to ½ **teaspoon crushed red pepper**
- 3 **tablespoons *each* chopped parsley and drained, chopped capers**
- 3 or 4 **anchovy fillets, finely chopped**
- 1 **can (2¼ oz.) sliced ripe olives, drained**
- ½ **cup dry white wine**
  Salt and pepper

Melt 5 tablespoons of the butter in a small pan; stir in 1 clove of the garlic. Brush over inside of each bread half. Stack breads, wrap in foil, and place in a 300° oven to warm.

Rinse chicken and pat dry; cut into ½-inch chunks. Place a wok or wide frying pan over medium-high heat. When pan is hot, add oil and remaining 1 tablespoon butter. When butter is melted, add remaining 2 cloves garlic, red pepper, and chicken; cook, stirring, until chicken is lightly browned (about 2 minutes). Stir in parsley, capers, anchovies, olives, and wine. Cook, stirring occasionally, until almost all liquid has evaporated

(about 5 minutes). Season to taste with salt and pepper.

Fill each bread half with about ⅙ of the chicken mixture. Makes about 3 servings.

Chicken Breasts with Papaya

Papaya chunks, lime juice, and chutney make a sweet, tangy foil for poultry in this stir-fry. You can serve it over rice if you wish, but we suggest spooning it over a bed of hot cooked spinach for extra color and flavor contrast. Use fresh or frozen spinach, and cook it just before you begin to stir-fry.

- ½ **cup sliced almonds**
- 3 **whole chicken breasts (about 1 lb. *each*), skinned, boned, and split (see page 93)**
- 1 **large papaya**
- 1½ **tablespoons lime or lemon juice**
- ½ **cup Major Grey's chutney, finely chopped**
- ½ **cup regular-strength chicken broth, homemade (page 53) or purchased**
- 1 **teaspoon cornstarch**
- ½ **teaspoon *each* paprika and ground ginger**
- 2 **tablespoons butter or margarine**
- 2 **tablespoons salad oil**
  White pepper
  Hot cooked spinach

Spread almonds in a shallow baking pan and toast in a 350° oven until golden (about 8 minutes). Set aside.

Rinse chicken and pat dry. Cut across the grain into ½-inch wide strips; set aside. Peel and halve papaya; remove seeds. Cut each half lengthwise into quarters, then cut each piece in half crosswise. Place in a bowl, add lime juice, and stir until fruit is coated. In another bowl, combine chutney, broth, cornstarch, paprika, and ginger.

Place a wok or 12-inch frying pan over medium-high heat. When pan is hot, add butter and oil. When butter is melted, add chicken and cook, stirring, until barely pink when slashed (about 5 minutes).

Stir chutney mixture and add to chicken. Bring to a boil and cook, stirring, until thickened (about 2 minutes). Add papaya and cook, stirring gently, just until fruit is glazed and heated through. Season to taste with pepper.

To serve, spoon chicken mixture over spinach; sprinkle with almonds. Makes 4 to 6 servings.

Experimental in composition but traditional in technique, Stir-fried
Chicken with Cheese (facing page) mingles chicken morsels with crunchy
bean sprouts, red bell pepper, peanuts, and pungent blue cheese.

Basic Stir-fried Chicken with Three Variations

You can vary this stir-fry to suit your fancy. Choose Peking, black bean, or sweet-sour sauce; each blends beautifully with the crisp vegetables and tender meat. If you stir-fry often, you can save a little time by doubling any of the sauces and storing the unused portion. Covered tightly and refrigerated, the sauces will keep up to 3 weeks.

Peking, Black Bean, or Sweet-Sour
Stir-fry Sauce (recipes follow)
1 large whole chicken breast (about 1½ lbs.), skinned, boned, and split (see page 93)
3 tablespoons salad oil
1 medium-size carrot, thinly sliced
½ small onion, thinly sliced
1 medium-size zucchini, thinly sliced
1 medium-size bell pepper, seeded and cut into thin strips
2 tablespoons water
1 tablespoon cornstarch

Prepare Peking, Black Bean, or Sweet-Sour Stir-fry Sauce and set aside.

Rinse chicken and pat dry; cut into ¾-inch chunks.

Place a wok or 12-inch frying pan over high heat. When pan is hot, add 2 tablespoons of the oil. When oil begins to heat, add chicken and cook, stirring, until no longer pink when slashed (3 to 5 minutes). Remove meat from pan.

Add remaining 1 tablespoon oil to pan. When oil begins to heat, add carrot and onion and cook, stirring, for 1 minute. Add zucchini, bell pepper, and water; cook, stirring, until vegetables are barely tender to bite (about 1½ more minutes).

Stir together cornstarch and sauce; pour into pan, then return meat to pan. Bring to a boil and cook, stirring, until thickened. Makes about 3 servings.

Peking Stir-fry Sauce. In a bowl, combine 1 clove **garlic**, minced or pressed; 2¼ teaspoons minced **fresh ginger**; ½ cup **water**; ¼ cup **hoisin sauce**; 2 tablespoons **soy sauce**; 1 tablespoon **white wine vinegar**; and 2½ teaspoons **sugar**.

Black Bean Stir-fry Sauce. Rinse, drain, and finely chop 2 tablespoons **fermented black beans**. Place beans in a small bowl; stir in 2¼ teaspoons minced **fresh ginger**; 2 cloves **garlic**, minced or pressed; 2 tablespoons *each* **dry sherry** and **soy sauce**; 1½ teaspoons **white wine vinegar**; ½ teaspoon **crushed red pepper**; and ¾ cup **water**.

Sweet-Sour Stir-fry Sauce. In a bowl, combine 2 cloves **garlic**, minced or pressed; 6 tablespoons **water**; ¼ cup *each* **sugar** and **cider vinegar**; 4 teaspoons *each* **dry sherry**, **soy sauce**, and minced **fresh ginger**; 1 tablespoon **catsup**; 2¼ teaspoons **sesame oil**; and ⅛ teaspoon **crushed red pepper**.

Stir-fried Chicken with Cheese

(Pictured on facing page)

Tangy blue cheese lends creaminess and unusual flavor to this entrée. Season with wasabi paste, if you like, but watch out—it's *hot*. (You'll find it in Asian markets and well-stocked supermarkets.)

1 pound chicken thighs (about 3), skinned
2½ tablespoons salad oil
½ cup raw shelled peanuts or unsalted dry-roasted peanuts
1 medium-size onion, thinly sliced
1 medium-size red bell pepper, seeded and cut into thin strips
2 cups bean sprouts
½ to 1 cup (2 to 4 oz.) coarsely crumbled blue-veined cheese
Soy sauce
Wasabi paste (optional)

Rinse chicken and pat dry. On inside of each thigh, cut meat to bone along entire length. With knife blade, scrape meat free from bone; then cut meat into 1-inch chunks.

Place a wok or 12-inch frying pan over medium-high heat. When pan is hot, add ½ tablespoon of the oil. When oil begins to heat, add peanuts; cook, stirring, until lightly toasted. Lift out and set aside.

Add remaining 2 tablespoons oil to pan. When oil is hot, add chicken; cook, stirring, until no longer pink when slashed (3 to 5 minutes). Lift out and set aside.

Add onion and bell pepper to pan and cook, stirring, until onion is tender-crisp to bite (about 2 minutes). Add bean sprouts, peanuts, and chicken; stir until heated through.

Pour chicken mixture into a serving dish and gently mix in cheese. At the table, pass soy and wasabi paste (if desired) to season individual portions. Makes about 2 servings.

Chinese Chicken Salad

Fresh cilantro gives this salad zip; peanuts and sesame seeds add a nutty flavor. The delicate crunch comes from deep-fried bean threads—thin, translucent noodles available in Asian markets and well-stocked supermarkets. Bean threads are packaged in tight bundles that are messy to separate. To avoid this problem, place bundles in a paper bag; then pull them apart, in the bag, into small sections.

   1 **whole chicken breast (about 1 lb.), split, and 2 chicken thighs (about ¾ lb.** *total***)**
   ¼ **cup all-purpose flour**
   ½ **teaspoon** *each* **Chinese five-spice and salt**
      Dash of pepper
   3 **ounces bean threads**
      Salad oil
      Dressing (recipe follows)
   ½ **cup sesame seeds**
   4 **cups finely shredded iceberg lettuce**
   3 **green onions (including tops), thinly sliced**
   1 **large bunch fresh cilantro (coriander), rinsed, stemmed, and finely chopped**
   1 **cup coarsely chopped salted peanuts**

Rinse chicken and pat dry. Stir flour, five-spice, salt, and pepper together on a large plate. Dredge chicken in flour mixture, turning to coat all sides; shake off excess. Set chicken aside.

Break bean threads into sections (see recipe introduction). In a wok or deep pan, heat 1½ inches of oil to 375°F on a deep-frying thermometer. Drop a handful of bean threads into oil. As bean threads puff and expand, push them down into oil with a wire skimmer or slotted spoon; then turn over entire mass. When bean threads stop crackling (about 30 seconds), lift them out with skimmer and drain on paper towels. Skim and discard any bits of bean threads from oil. Repeat with remaining bean threads. (At this point, you may cool bean threads completely, then package airtight and store at room temperature until next day.)

If necessary, bring oil temperature back to 375°F. Lower chicken into oil; cook, turning after 5 or 6 minutes, until meat near bone is no longer pink when slashed (about 10 minutes *total* for breasts, 12 minutes *total* for thighs). Drain on paper towels; set aside and let cool. Meanwhile, prepare Dressing.

Cut chicken and skin off bones, then cut into bite-size pieces. (At this point, you may cover chicken and dressing and refrigerate separately until next day.)

Pour sesame seeds into a wide frying pan. Toast over medium heat until golden, stirring often (about 5 minutes). Set aside and let cool.

Place lettuce in a large serving bowl; top with onions, cilantro, and chicken. Sprinkle with sesame seeds and peanuts. Stir Dressing, then drizzle over salad and toss. Add bean threads, lightly crushing some of them with your hands; toss lightly. Serve immediately (noodles soften quickly with standing). Makes 4 servings.

Dressing. In a small bowl, combine ¾ teaspoon **dry mustard**, 1 teaspoon *each* **sugar** and grated **lemon peel**, 1 tablespoon *each* **soy sauce** and **lemon juice**, and ¼ cup **salad oil**.

Chicken & Vegetable Tempura

Serve crisp, lacy tempura immediately after cooking; the fragile coating softens upon standing.

   1 **large chicken breast (about 1½ lbs.), skinned, boned, and split (see page 93)**
      Vegetables (suggestions follow)
      Tempura Dipping Sauce (recipe follows)
   3 **tablespoons shredded fresh ginger**
   3 **tablespoons shredded daikon**
      Salad oil
      Tempura Batter (recipe follows)

Rinse chicken, then cut with the grain into ½ by 3-inch strips. Pat very dry. Prepare vegetables and arrange on a platter with chicken. Prepare dipping sauce; pour into 4 small bowls. Place ginger and daikon in separate small bowls.

In a wok or deep pan, heat 2 inches of oil to 375°F on a deep-frying thermometer. Meanwhile, prepare batter.

Using tongs, dip chicken and vegetables, one piece at a time, into batter. Let excess batter drip off, then gently lower into hot oil (cook several pieces at a time; do not crowd in pan). Cook, turning occasionally, until crisp and light golden (2½ to 3 minutes). Remove and let drain briefly on a wire rack. Serve at once, with sauce for dipping; let diners add ginger and daikon to sauce according to taste. As you fry, frequently skim and discard any bits of batter from oil. Makes about 3 servings.

Vegetables. Choose at least 3 of the following: 2 medium-size **carrots,** cut into 2½ to 3-inch lengths, then into ¼-inch-thick lengthwise slices; ⅓-pound wedge of a large **eggplant,** cut crosswise into ¼-inch-thick slices; 12 large **mushrooms,** cut in half lengthwise; 1 medium-size **sweet potato,** peeled and cut into ¼-inch-thick rounds; and ¼ pound **green beans,** ends removed (cut in half if long).

Tempura Dipping Sauce. In a small pan, combine 1 cup **regular-strength chicken broth,** homemade (page 53) or purchased, and ¼ cup *each* **soy sauce** and **dry sherry.** Bring to a boil over medium-high heat; then remove from heat and let cool to room temperature.

Tempura Batter. In a small bowl, lightly beat 1 cup plus 2 tablespoons **ice cold water, 1 egg,** and ¼ teaspoon *each* **baking soda** and **salt.** Add 1 cup unsifted **cake flour;** mix just until blended (batter will be lumpy). Sprinkle another ⅓ cup unsifted **cake flour** over top of batter. With a fork, stir batter 1 or 2 strokes (do not blend thoroughly; most of last addition of flour should be floating on top). Half-fill a larger bowl with **ice;** set bowl of batter in it to keep batter cold.

Crisp Chicken Nuggets

Some people like chicken nuggets for their crunchy crust and juicy meat. Others think the dipping sauces are what makes them so good. Whatever the reason, these crisp morsels are sure to please.

You'll need about 2 cups dipping sauce to accompany the nuggets. Each sauce recipe makes about 1 cup, so you can either double your favorite recipe or prepare two sauces. (Or prepare a half recipe of all five sauces.)

>   Dipping sauces (recipes follow)
> 3 **whole chicken breasts (about 1 lb. *each*),** skinned, boned, and split (see page 93); or **10 chicken thighs (about 3 lbs. *total*),** skinned
> 1 **cup all-purpose flour**
> ½ **teaspoon paprika**
> 1 **teaspoon salt**
> ⅛ **teaspoon pepper**
> ¾ **cup beer**
>   **Salad oil**

Prepare sauces of your choice; set aside. Rinse chicken and pat dry. If using thighs, cut meat to bone along entire length on inside of each thigh. With knife blade, scrape meat free from bone. Cut breast or thigh meat into 1½-inch chunks.

In a large bowl, stir together flour, paprika, salt, and pepper with a wire whisk. Gradually whisk in beer, blending until smooth.

In a deep pan, heat 2 inches of oil to 350°F on a deep-frying thermometer. Place chicken in batter and stir to coat. Using tongs, lower about 8 pieces of chicken, one at a time, into oil. Cook until meat in center is no longer pink when slashed (about 4 minutes). If nuggets stick together while cooking, gently break apart with the side of a spoon. Lift nuggets from oil with a slotted spoon, drain on paper towels, and keep warm. Repeat with remaining chicken. Serve warm, with sauces for dipping. Makes about 3½ dozen (about 6 servings).

Teriyaki Sauce. Prepare **Teriyaki Sauce** (page 10).

Barbecue Sauce. Prepare **Basic Barbecue Sauce** (page 43).

Sweet-Sour Sauce. Prepare **Sweet-Sour Stir-fry Sauce** (page 31), but mix it up in a 1 to 2-quart pan and stir in 1 tablespoon **cornstarch.** Cook over medium heat, stirring, until sauce boils and thickens.

Dijon Sauce. In a small bowl, stir together ¾ cup **sour cream,** ¼ cup **Dijon mustard,** 1½ teaspoons **lemon juice,** and ¼ teaspoon **pepper.**

Horseradish Mayonnaise. Stir together ¾ cup **mayonnaise,** 6 to 7 tablespoons **prepared horseradish,** and 1 tablespoon **lemon juice.**

Mexican-style Chicken Nuggets

Prepare **Crisp Chicken Nuggets,** but decrease flour in batter to ¾ cup. To flour mixture add ¼ cup **cornmeal,** 2 teaspoons **chili powder,** and ¼ teaspoon *each* **ground cumin** and **oregano leaves.** Serve with **Guacamole Dip** (below). (One recipe Guacamole Dip makes enough to accompany a full recipe of nuggets.)

Guacamole Dip. Halve and pit 2 medium-size **avocados,** then scoop pulp into a small bowl. Mash pulp; stir in ¼ cup **sour cream** or plain yogurt, 2 tablespoons **lemon or lime juice,** 2 tablespoons chopped **fresh cilantro (coriander) leaves,** ½ teaspoon **ground cumin,** and 2 to 4 tablespoons **canned diced green chiles.** Season to taste with **salt** and **liquid hot pepper seasoning.**

Herb & Cheese Nuggets

Prepare **Crisp Chicken Nuggets,** but decrease salt in batter to ¾ teaspoon. To flour mixture add 3 tablespoons grated **Parmesan cheese** and ½ teaspoon *each* **dry basil, dry rosemary, thyme leaves,** and **oregano leaves.** Omit sauces; instead, serve **lemon wedges** to squeeze over nuggets.

Backyard Barbecues

Chicken cooked over coals

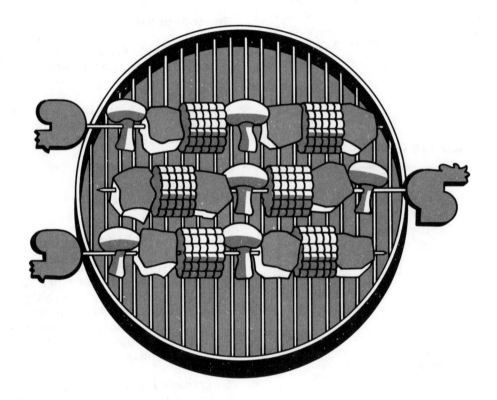

For centuries, cooks and diners have appreciated the smoky aroma and flavor of birds grilled over an open fire. Cooking chicken outdoors inspires a festive mood, whether the occasion is a leisurely cookout or a quick after-work meal.

On the following pages, you'll find recipes as varied as these occasions—whole birds grilled slowly with the indirect heat of a covered barbecue, as well as chicken pieces and spicy kebabs that cook more quickly on an open grill. (For ideas on grilling duck, turkey, and other birds, check the index.)

In addition to the barbecue itself, you'll need some basic equipment: long-handled tongs, thick oven mitts, bamboo or metal skewers, aluminum drip pans, and a metal brush for cleaning the cooking grill. You will also need an electric starter, fire chimney, or other type of starter for lighting the charcoal.

Though barbecuing isn't difficult, getting consistent results requires knowing how to start the fire and keep it at an even temperature. To get the uninitiated off to a good start, we give basic guidelines for grilling with both indirect and direct heat (see pages 37 and 39).

Onion-stuffed Chicken

Herb-seasoned tiny onions fill this bird, flavoring the meat as it cooks.

    3½ to 4-pound whole frying chicken
1   clove garlic, cut in half
1   can (16 oz.) small whole onions, drained
2   bay leaves
¼   cup butter or margarine, melted
½   teaspoon pepper
¼   teaspoon *each* thyme, oregano, and
    marjoram leaves
¼   teaspoon *each* dry basil and rubbed sage
2   tablespoons dry sherry

About 45 minutes before cooking, start barbecue fire (see "Barbecuing with Indirect Heat," page 37).

Remove chicken neck and giblets; reserve for other uses, if desired. Discard lumps of fat. Rinse chicken inside and out; pat dry. Rub cut sides of garlic over chicken skin, then put garlic in body cavity with onions and bay leaves.

Combine butter, pepper, thyme, oregano, marjoram, basil, sage, and sherry. Spoon 1 tablespoon of the mixture into body cavity; reserve remainder for basting. Truss both cavities; bend wings akimbo (see page 65). Brush all over with butter mixture.

Place chicken, breast down, in middle of grill over drip pan. Cover barbecue, adjust dampers, and cook for 30 minutes. Baste chicken with butter mixture; then turn breast up and continue to cook, basting occasionally, until a meat thermometer inserted in thickest portion of thigh (not touching bone) registers 185°F or until meat near thighbone is no longer pink when slashed (30 to 45 more minutes). Spoon stuffing into a serving bowl; offer with chicken. Makes 4 or 5 servings.

Easy Barbecued Chicken

For a minimum-effort meal, serve small chickens simply seasoned with celery seeds and vinegar.

2   whole frying chickens (3 to 3½ lbs. *each*)
    Celery seeds, paprika, garlic powder,
    and pepper
3   tablespoons *each* cider vinegar and
    salad oil

About 45 minutes before cooking, start barbecue fire (see "Barbecuing with Indirect Heat," page 37).

Remove chicken necks and giblets; reserve for other uses, if desired. Discard lumps of fat. Rinse chickens inside and out; pat dry, then sprinkle all over with celery seeds, paprika, garlic powder, and pepper. Rub seasonings into skin. Bend wings akimbo (see page 65).

Place chickens, breast down, in middle of grill over drip pan. Cover barbecue, adjust dampers, and cook for 20 minutes. Mix vinegar and oil; brush over chickens. Cook for 10 more minutes; turn chickens breast up and continue to cook, brushing often with vinegar mixture, until a meat thermometer inserted in thickest portion of thigh (not touching bone) registers 185°F or until meat near thighbone is no longer pink when slashed (30 to 40 more minutes). Makes about 8 servings.

Cilantro & Sake Roast Chicken

Sake and fresh cilantro complement the smoke-tinged flavor of barbecued chicken.

    3½ to 4-pound whole frying chicken
    Pepper
1   cup chopped celery leaves
1   cup chopped fresh cilantro (coriander)
8   fresh rosemary sprigs (*each* about
    2 inches long) or ¾ teaspoon
    dry rosemary
½   cup sake

Remove chicken neck and giblets; reserve for other uses, if desired. Discard lumps of fat. Rinse chicken inside and out; pat dry. Sprinkle both cavities with pepper.

In a bowl, combine celery leaves, cilantro, rosemary, and ¼ cup of the sake. Stuff mixture into body cavity of chicken; then truss both cavities and bend wings akimbo (see page 65). Cover chicken and refrigerate for 1 hour.

About 45 minutes before cooking, start barbecue fire (see "Barbecuing with Indirect Heat," page 37). Place chicken, breast down, in middle of grill over drip pan. Cover barbecue, adjust dampers, and cook for 30 minutes; then turn chicken breast up and continue to cook, brushing several times with remaining ¼ cup sake, until a meat thermometer inserted in thickest portion of thigh (not touching bone) registers 185°F or until meat near thighbone is no longer pink when slashed (30 to 45 more minutes). Remove chicken from barbecue; discard stuffing, then transfer chicken to a platter. Pass pan drippings to spoon over individual portions. Makes 4 or 5 servings.

Peach-glazed Chicken

In midsummer, barbecue chefs are out in full force, and peaches are at their ripest and juiciest. This coincidence makes for extra tasty chicken dishes—such as this roaster with a curried peach glaze.

    5 to 6-pound roasting chicken
½   teaspoon marjoram leaves
¼   teaspoon pepper
3   large ripe peaches, peeled, pitted, and diced
¼   cup *each* firmly packed brown sugar and orange juice
1   tablespoon grated orange peel
2   tablespoons minced crystallized ginger
1   green onion (including top), chopped
3   tablespoons dry white wine
¾   teaspoon curry powder

About 45 minutes before cooking, start barbecue fire (see "Barbecuing with Indirect Heat," facing page).

Remove chicken neck and giblets; reserve for other uses, if desired. Discard lumps of fat. Rinse chicken inside and out; pat dry. Sprinkle both cavities with marjoram and pepper; then truss chicken and bend wings akimbo (see page 65). Place chicken, breast down, in middle of grill over drip pan. Cover barbecue, adjust dampers, and cook for 1 hour.

Meanwhile, in a 3 to 4-quart pan, combine peaches, sugar, orange juice, orange peel, ginger, onion, wine, and curry powder. Cook over medium-high heat until bubbly; then reduce heat and boil gently, uncovered, until thickened (15 to 20 minutes). Stir often to prevent sticking.

Turn chicken breast up, brush generously with peach mixture, and continue to cook until a meat thermometer inserted in thickest portion of thigh (not touching bone) registers 185°F or until meat near thighbone is no longer pink when slashed (30 to 45 more minutes). Offer remaining peach mixture to spoon over individual portions. Makes 6 or 7 servings.

Chicken with Spinach-Rice Stuffing

Extra stuffing can be heated separately and used either as a side dish or as a decorative bed for this onion-basted grilled bird.

Spinach-Rice Stuffing (recipe follows)
3½ to 4-pound whole frying chicken
Green Onion Butter (page 43)

Prepare Spinach-Rice Stuffing; set aside. About 45 minutes before cooking, start barbecue fire (see "Barbecuing with Indirect Heat," facing page).

Remove chicken neck and giblets; reserve for other uses, if desired. Discard lumps of fat. Rinse chicken inside and out and pat dry; then stuff both cavities with Spinach-Rice Stuffing. Truss chicken and bend wings akimbo (see page 65). Spoon remaining stuffing into a greased 9 by 5-inch loaf pan. Cover with foil. Bake in a 425° oven during last 25 minutes of barbecuing time.

Prepare Green Onion Butter. Place chicken, breast down, in middle of grill over drip pan. Brush with Green Onion Butter. Cover barbecue, adjust dampers, and cook for 30 minutes. Brush again with Green Onion Butter; then turn chicken breast up. Continue to cook, brushing occasionally with Green Onion Butter, until a meat thermometer inserted in thickest portion of thigh (not touching bone) registers 185°F or until meat near thighbone is no longer pink when slashed (30 to 45 more minutes). Makes 4 or 5 servings.

Spinach-Rice Stuffing. Heat 2 tablespoons **salad oil** in a wide frying pan over medium-high heat. Add 4 cups thinly sliced **spinach** leaves (about ¾ lb., stems removed); 1 can (8 oz.) **water chestnuts,** drained and slivered; and ½ cup *each* minced **green onions** (including tops) and diced **celery.** Cook, stirring, until spinach is wilted (about 3 minutes); remove from heat. Add 2 cups **cooked rice** and ¼ teaspoon **dry rosemary;** season to taste with **salt** and **pepper.** Let cool. Makes 4⅓ cups.

Mediterranean Fruited Chicken

This lemony Greek-style chicken is served with a garland of orange and avocado slices.

    5 to 6-pound roasting chicken
    Lemon-Herb Marinade
    (recipe follows)
1   lemon
1   small onion
2   large oranges
1   avocado
1   tablespoon lemon juice

Remove chicken neck and giblets; reserve for other uses, if desired. Discard lumps of fat. Rinse chicken inside and out; pat dry. Prepare Lemon-Herb Marinade. Place chicken in bowl with marinade and turn to coat; then cover and refrigerate for 2 hours, turning occasionally.

About 45 minutes before cooking, start barbecue fire (see "Barbecuing with Indirect Heat," at right). Lift chicken from marinade and drain briefly (reserve marinade). Cut lemon into wedges and onion into quarters, then place both in body cavity. Truss both cavities and bend wings akimbo (see page 65).

Place chicken, breast down, in middle of grill over drip pan. Cover barbecue, adjust dampers, and cook for 1 hour; then turn chicken breast up and continue to cook, basting several times with marinade, until a meat thermometer inserted in thickest portion of thigh (not touching bone) registers 185°F or until meat near thighbone is no longer pink when slashed (30 to 45 more minutes).

Remove chicken from barbecue; discard lemon and onion, then transfer chicken to a platter. Peel and thinly slice oranges. Pit, peel, and slice avocado; sprinkle with lemon juice. Garnish chicken with oranges and avocado. Makes 6 or 7 servings.

Lemon-Herb Marinade. In a large bowl, mix ⅓ cup *each* **fresh lemon juice, dry white wine,** and **olive oil;** 1 teaspoon *each* **salt** and **oregano leaves;** ½ teaspoon *each* **dry tarragon, dry rosemary,** and **pepper;** and 3 cloves **garlic,** minced or pressed.

Chicken Provençal

Mustard mixed with garlic, wine, and herbs makes a savory coating for whole chicken legs.

- 2 tablespoons Dijon mustard
- 1 teaspoon Italian herb seasoning
- 2 teaspoons dry white wine
- 1½ tablespoons minced onion
- 1 clove garlic, minced or pressed
- 6 whole chicken legs, thighs attached (about 3 lbs. *total*), rinsed and patted dry

Mix mustard, herb seasoning, wine, onion, and garlic until smooth; spread evenly over all sides of chicken. Cover and refrigerate for 2 to 4 hours.

About 45 minutes before cooking, start barbecue fire (see "Barbecuing with Direct Heat," page 39). Place chicken on grill 4 to 6 inches above a solid bed of low-glowing coals. Cook, turning frequently, until meat near thighbone is no longer pink when slashed (40 to 50 minutes). Makes 6 servings.

Barbecuing with Indirect Heat

Whole birds require slow, even cooking, and that's just what the indirect heat of a covered barbecue gives them. The bird sits on the cooking grill, over a drip pan set on the fire grate; hot coals are banked on each side of the pan. When the cover is in place, heat is reflected onto the meat, providing the same even cooking as an oven does. Either a kettle or a box-shaped barbecue is suitable for this type of barbecuing. If your barbecue has a spit attachment, you can also use it to roast whole poultry; follow the manufacturer's directions.

To barbecue, follow these steps: Open or remove lid from barbecue; then open bottom dampers. Pile about 40 long-burning briquets on fire grate and ignite. Let briquets burn to the "glowing" stage (30 to 40 minutes—see page 39). Using long-handled tongs, bank about half the briquets on each side of fire grate; place a metal drip pan in center.

Set cooking grill in place 4 to 6 inches above pan. Lightly grease grill; set bird on grill, breast down, directly above pan.

Cover barbecue; adjust dampers as necessary to maintain an even heat. Cook for about half the total time specified in recipe; then turn bird over. Continue to cook until a meat thermometer inserted in thickest portion of thigh (not touching bone) registers 185°F or until meat near thighbone is no longer pink when slashed.

To keep temperature constant during cooking, add 5 or 6 briquets to each side of fire grate every 30 to 45 minutes.

Grilled Chicken with Bay, Squash & Tomatoes

Bay leaves and a vinaigrette flavor skewered chicken thighs, summer squash, and tomatoes.

    12 chicken thighs (about 4 lbs. *total*)
     3 tablespoons *each* Dijon mustard and
       white wine vinegar
    ¾ cup olive oil or salad oil
     1 teaspoon coarsely ground pepper
       About 36 fresh bay leaves (or dry bay
       leaves soaked in hot water for 1 hour)
     4 medium-size crookneck squash, cut into
       ½-inch-thick slices
     3 cups cherry tomatoes, stemmed

Skin chicken, if desired; then rinse and pat dry. In a large bowl, stir together mustard, vinegar, oil, pepper, and 6 of the bay leaves. Add chicken and turn to coat. Cover and refrigerate for at least 6 hours or until next day, turning chicken several times.

About 40 minutes before cooking, start barbecue fire (see "Barbecuing with Direct Heat," facing page). Lift chicken from marinade and drain briefly. Add squash to marinade and turn to coat; then lift out squash and bay leaves and discard marinade.

You will need 9 metal skewers, each about 10 inches long. On 3 of the skewers, alternate chicken with 12 of the bay leaves (including those from marinade). On 3 more skewers, thread squash, piercing it through skin, and about half the remaining bay leaves. Thread tomatoes and remaining bay leaves on remaining 3 skewers.

Place chicken on grill 4 to 6 inches above a solid bed of medium-glowing coals. Cook, turning frequently, for 10 minutes. Place squash on grill. Continue to cook, turning squash and chicken often, until meat near thighbone is no longer pink when slashed (20 to 30 more minutes). Set tomatoes on grill about 5 minutes before chicken is done; cook, turning, until hot throughout. Makes 6 servings.

Chicken & Fruit Kebabs

(Pictured on page 3)

Juicy chunks of pineapple and papaya pair beautifully with sherry- and soy-flavored chicken. You thread the fruit on skewers and start the chicken marinating in advance; actual cooking time is less than 15 minutes.

     2 tablespoons sesame seeds
     3 large whole chicken breasts (about
       1½ lbs. *each*), skinned, boned, and
       split (see page 93)
       Sherry-Soy Marinade (recipe follows)
     1 large papaya, peeled, seeded, and cut
       into 1½-inch chunks
     1 small pineapple (3 to 3½ lbs.), peeled,
       cored, and cut into 1½-inch chunks

Toast sesame seeds in a small frying pan over medium heat, stirring often, until golden (about 5 minutes). Set aside.

Rinse chicken and pat dry. Cut each breast half into 6 or 7 equal-size chunks. Prepare Sherry-Soy Marinade. Pour ¼ cup of the marinade into a bowl; reserve remaining marinade. Add chicken to marinade in bowl and mix gently to coat. Cover and let stand for 1 hour; or refrigerate for up to 8 hours.

About 45 minutes before cooking, start barbecue fire (see "Barbecuing with Direct Heat," facing page). Lift chicken from marinade and drain briefly (discard marinade left in bowl). Thread chicken on 6 bamboo or metal skewers (each about 12 inches long). Thread fruit on 6 more skewers, alternating papaya and pineapple on each skewer.

Place chicken on grill 4 to 6 inches above a solid bed of low-glowing coals. Cook, turning occasionally, until meat is no longer pink when slashed (10 to 12 minutes).

Meanwhile, brush fruit with a little of the reserved marinade. Place on grill next to chicken and cook, turning occasionally, just until heated through and lightly browned (about 3 minutes).

To serve, sprinkle chicken and fruit with some of the marinade, then with sesame seeds. Accompany with any remaining marinade. Makes about 6 servings.

Sherry-Soy Marinade. Stir together ⅓ cup **dry sherry**, 3 tablespoons *each* **soy sauce** and **sesame oil**, and 1½ teaspoons finely chopped **fresh ginger**.

Yucatán Chicken

Tart Seville orange juice mixed with herbs and spices makes *escabeche* paste, a seasoning mixture used in Mexico's Yucatán region. Since Seville oranges aren't generally available in the United States, we've substituted a half-and-half mixture of orange juice and vinegar.

    3 to 3½-pound frying chicken, cut up
    Escabeche Paste (recipe follows)

Reserve chicken neck and giblets for other uses, if desired. Rinse chicken and pat dry. Prepare Escabeche Paste. Pierce chicken all over with the tip of a sharp knife; then rub paste over chicken, pushing some under skin. Cover and refrigerate for at least 2 hours or until next day.

About 45 minutes before cooking, start barbecue fire (see "Barbecuing with Direct Heat," at right). Place chicken, skin side up, on grill 4 to 6 inches above a solid bed of low-glowing coals. Cook, turning occasionally, until meat near bone is no longer pink when slashed (40 to 50 minutes for dark meat, about 30 minutes for white meat). Makes about 4 servings.

Escabeche Paste. In a bowl, stir together 4 cloves **garlic,** minced or pressed; ½ teaspoon *each* **ground allspice, cloves, cumin, coriander,** and coarsely ground **pepper;** ¾ teaspoon **ground cinnamon;** 1 teaspoon **oregano leaves;** ⅛ teaspoon **ground red pepper** (cayenne); and 1 tablespoon *each* **orange juice** and **white wine vinegar.**

Tandoori Chicken with Yogurt

This spicy North Indian chicken gets its name from *tandoor*—the bucketlike, charcoal-fired oven in which it's traditionally cooked.

- 4 **whole chicken legs, thighs attached (about 2 lbs. *total*)**
- 1 **teaspoon *each* grated fresh ginger and ground allspice**
- ¼ **to ½ teaspoon crushed red pepper**
- 2 **cloves garlic, minced or pressed**
- 1 **tablespoon lemon juice**
  Plain yogurt

About 40 minutes before cooking, start barbecue fire (see "Barbecuing with Direct Heat," at right). Rinse chicken and pat dry. In a bowl, mash together ginger, allspice, pepper, garlic, and lemon juice to make a paste. Then lift skin of each chicken leg; spread 1 teaspoon paste over flesh of thigh and top of drumstick. Brush any remaining paste evenly over skin.

Place chicken, skin side up, on grill 4 to 6 inches above a solid bed of medium-glowing coals. Cook, turning frequently, until meat near thighbone is no longer pink when slashed (30 to 40 minutes). Pass cold yogurt to spoon over chicken. Makes 4 servings.

Barbecuing with Direct Heat

Outdoor cooks have traditionally relied on built-in barbecues, braziers, hibachis, and other open grills for barbecuing with direct heat. More and more, however, the kettle barbecue is being used for direct-heat barbecuing—though many manufacturers advise keeping the kettle covered when it's being used this way.

To barbecue, follow these steps: Open bottom dampers if your barbecue has them. Spread long-burning briquets on fire grate in a solid layer 1 to 2 inches wider than grill area required for food. Then mound charcoal and ignite.

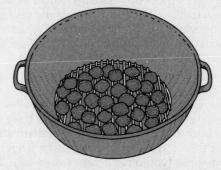

Fire temperatures are usually described as glowing, medium-glowing, or low-glowing. **Glowing** describes the hottest fire; coals are just covered with gray ash. **Medium-glowing** coals glow through a layer of gray ash; **low-glowing** coals are thickly covered with gray ash.

When coals have reached the desired temperature, spread them out again in a single, solid layer. Set grill in place at recommended height above coals; grease lightly. Place food on grill and cook (basting, if recipe directs) until meat near bone is no longer pink when slashed. Watch foods carefully and turn them often to avoid overcooking. Adjust dampers to regulate fire temperature.

If you're using a marinade or baste that contains sugar or ingredients high in sugar (such as catsup or fruit), apply it during the last part of cooking and turn frequently to prevent scorching. Also have a water mister handy to extinguish any flare-ups.

Malihini Barbecue

Malihini—Hawaiian for "newcomer"—is an appropriate term for our whole-meal, party-menu recipe. It combines the sweetness of tropical fruits with the fire of Asian curry, bringing together foreign flavors which have become important in Island cuisine.

> Curried Coconut Cream Sauce
> (recipe follows)
> 16 chicken drumsticks (about 4 lbs. *total*)
> Condiments (suggestions follow)
> About 6 cups hot cooked rice
> 1 small ripe pineapple (3 to 3½ lbs.),
> peeled and cut crosswise into 6 slices
> 8 green onions (including tops), cut into
> 2-inch lengths, then slivered
> Small dried hot red chiles (optional)

Prepare Curried Coconut Cream Sauce. Pour 1 cup of the sauce into a large bowl; cover and refrigerate remaining sauce. Rinse chicken, pat dry, and add to sauce in bowl; stir, then cover and refrigerate for at least 4 hours or until next day.

About 45 minutes before cooking, start barbecue fire (see "Barbecuing with Direct Heat," page 39). Thread 4 drumsticks on a pair of parallel 10 to 12-inch-long bamboo or metal skewers; have one skewer running through bony end of drumsticks, the other through meaty end. Repeat with remaining drumsticks (you'll need 8 skewers *total*). Rub sauce left in bowl onto skewered chicken.

Place chicken on grill 4 to 6 inches above a solid bed of low-glowing coals. Cook, turning occasionally, until meat near bone is no longer pink when slashed (40 to 50 minutes).

Meanwhile, prepare condiments; then warm remaining sauce in a 1 to 2-quart pan over medium heat, stirring frequently. Pour sauce into a serving bowl.

To serve, place rice and pineapple on individual plates; slide chicken from skewers onto plates. Top all with sauce, then spoon condiments and onions alongside. If you wish, crumble chiles over chicken for added heat. Makes 5 or 6 servings.

Curried Coconut Cream Sauce. Melt 3 tablespoons **butter** or margarine in a wide frying pan over medium-high heat. Add 2 medium-size **onions,** chopped; 1 clove **garlic,** minced or pressed; and 1 tablespoon minced **fresh ginger.** Cook, stirring, until onions are soft. Stir in 2 tablespoons **all-purpose flour,** 4½ teaspoons **curry powder,** 1½ teaspoons **sugar,** and ¼ teaspoon **crushed red pepper;** cook, stirring, for 1 minute.

Remove from heat and smoothly blend in 2 cans (12 to 14 oz. *each*) **unsweetened coconut milk,** thawed if frozen. (As an alternate to coconut milk, mix 3 cups half-and-half (light cream) with 1½ teaspoons *each* sugar and coconut extract.) Then bring to a boil over medium heat, stirring frequently. Continue to cook, uncovered, until sauce is reduced to about 3 cups (about 15 minutes); stir frequently. Season to taste with **salt.**

Condiments. Choose at least 3 of the following: ¾ cup coarsely chopped **macadamia nuts;** ¾ cup **unsweetened flaked coconut;** ¾ cup coarsely chopped **Major Grey's chutney;** ¾ cup lightly packed **fresh cilantro (coriander) leaves;** and 2 medium size firm-ripe **bananas,** thinly sliced and mixed with 2 teaspoons **lemon juice.**

Rosemary Chicken Quarters

For best flavor, start this chicken marinating at least 3 hours before you barbecue.

> 3 to 3½-pound frying chicken, quartered
> ½ cup olive oil or salad oil
> 2 teaspoons dry rosemary
> 1 teaspoon finely chopped parsley
> 2 cloves garlic, minced or pressed
> 2 tablespoons lemon juice
> ⅛ teaspoon pepper

Reserve chicken neck and giblets for other uses, if desired. Rinse chicken and pat dry. In a large bowl, combine oil, rosemary, parsley, garlic, lemon juice, and pepper. Turn chicken in marinade to coat. Cover and refrigerate for at least 3 hours or until next day, turning occasionally.

About 45 minutes before cooking, start barbecue fire (see "Barbecuing with Direct Heat," page 39). Lift chicken from marinade and drain briefly (reserve marinade). Place chicken, skin side up, on grill 4 to 6 inches above a solid bed of low-glowing coals. Cook, turning and basting with marinade, until meat near thighbone is no longer pink when slashed (40 to 50 minutes). Makes 4 servings.

Garlic-basted Chicken

Many people insist that garlic is "good for what ails you." We know it's good for flavoring chicken, especially when combined with the subtle hop overtones from beer.

> 6 **whole chicken legs, thighs attached (about 3 lbs. *total*); or 3 whole chicken breasts (about 1 lb. *each*), split**
> ½ **cup (¼ lb.) butter or margarine**
> 4 **cloves garlic, minced or pressed**
> ¼ **cup finely chopped onion**
> 1 **cup beer**
> 1 **tablespoon finely chopped parsley**
> ½ **teaspoon coarsely ground pepper**

About 45 minutes before cooking, start barbecue fire (see "Barbecuing with Direct Heat," page 39).

Rinse chicken and pat dry. Melt butter in a small pan over medium heat; add garlic and onion and cook, stirring occasionally, until onion is soft. Add beer and bring to a boil, stirring. Remove from heat. Stir in parsley and pepper; pour into a large bowl. Turn chicken in butter mixture to coat; lift out and drain briefly (reserve butter mixture).

Place chicken, skin side up, on grill 4 to 6 inches above a solid bed of low-glowing coals. Cook, turning and basting frequently with butter mixture, until meat near thighbone is no longer pink when slashed (40 to 50 minutes) or until breast is no longer pink when slashed in thickest part (about 30 minutes). Makes 6 servings.

Ginger Chicken Quarters

A teriyaki-style blend of soy, sherry, and ginger does triple duty in this recipe—first as a marinade, then as a baste, and finally, slightly thickened, as a sauce to spoon over chicken and rice.

> 3 **to 3½-pound frying chicken, quartered**
> ⅓ **cup soy sauce**
> 1 **cup water**
> 1 **clove garlic, minced or pressed**
> 1 **tablespoon sugar**
> 2 **tablespoons dry sherry**
> 3 **tablespoons minced fresh ginger**
> **Hot cooked rice**
> ¼ **cup sesame seeds**
> 2 **teaspoons *each* cornstarch and water**

Reserve chicken neck and giblets for other uses, if desired. Rinse chicken and pat dry. In a large bowl, combine soy, water, garlic, sugar, sherry, and ginger. Turn chicken in marinade to coat. Cover and refrigerate for at least 4 hours or until next day, turning occasionally.

About 45 minutes before cooking, start barbecue fire (see "Barbecuing with Direct Heat," page 39). Lift chicken from marinade and drain briefly. Reserve ½ cup of the marinade for a baste; set remainder aside for sauce. Place chicken, skin side up, on grill 4 to 6 inches above a solid bed of low-glowing coals. Cook, turning and basting frequently with the ½ cup reserved marinade, until meat near thighbone is no longer pink when slashed (40 to 50 minutes). Arrange chicken and rice on a platter and keep warm.

In a wide frying pan over medium heat, toast sesame seeds until golden (about 5 minutes), stirring often. Pour in remaining marinade. Combine cornstarch and water, then stir into marinade mixture; cook, stirring, until thickened. Spoon over chicken and rice. Makes 4 servings.

Chili-glazed Chicken with Peas

Lime, garlic, and chili powder make a tangy baste for chicken. Accompany the meat with peas in the pod, steamed in a heavy pan set on the barbecue (or use tiny frozen peas, cooked on the range).

> 3 **to 3½-pound frying chicken, cut up**
> ⅓ **cup butter or margarine**
> 2 **cloves garlic, minced or pressed**
> 1 **teaspoon chili powder**
> ¼ **teaspoon *each* ground cumin and grated lime peel**
> 2 **tablespoons lime juice**
> 2 **pounds peas in the pod**
> 2 **tablespoons water**

About 45 minutes before cooking, start barbecue fire (see "Barbecuing with Direct Heat," page 39). Reserve chicken neck and giblets for other uses, if desired. Rinse chicken and pat dry. Melt butter in a small pan over medium heat; remove from heat and stir in garlic, chili powder, cumin, lime peel, and lime juice. Generously brush over chicken.

Place chicken, skin side up, on grill 4 to 6 inches above a solid bed of low-glowing coals. Cook, turning and basting frequently with butter mixture, until meat near bone is no longer pink when slashed (40 to 50 minutes for dark meat, about 30 minutes for white meat).

Meanwhile, rinse peas; then place in a cast-iron frying pan or Dutch oven and add water. Cover with lid or foil; place on grill next to chicken during last 15 minutes of cooking, stirring peas every 5 minutes. Let guests shell their own peas to eat alongside chicken. Makes about 4 servings.

Barbecued Herb-Mustard Chicken

If you're a mustard fan, you might try varying the spicy marinade for this chicken by using different mustards—Dijon, tarragon, green peppercorn, hot English-style, and German coarse-grained mustard are all possibilities.

    3 to 3½-pound frying chicken, cut up
½   cup dry white wine
⅔   cup salad oil
6   tablespoons wine vinegar
2   tablespoons finely chopped onion
1   teaspoon Italian herb seasoning or thyme leaves
2   cloves garlic, minced or pressed
½   teaspoon pepper
¼   cup spicy brown mustard

Reserve chicken neck and giblets for other uses, if desired. Rinse chicken and pat dry. In a bowl, combine wine, oil, vinegar, onion, herb seasoning, garlic, pepper, and mustard. Turn chicken in marinade to coat. Cover and refrigerate for at least 4 hours or until next day, turning occasionally.

About 45 minutes before cooking, start barbecue fire (see "Barbecuing with Direct Heat," page 39). Lift chicken from marinade and drain briefly (reserve marinade). Place chicken, skin side up, on grill 4 to 6 inches above a solid bed of low-glowing coals. Cook, turning and basting frequently with marinade, until meat near bone is no longer pink when slashed (40 to 50 minutes for dark meat, about 30 minutes for white meat). Makes about 4 servings.

Savory Herb Chicken

Sherry, garlic, and four kinds of herbs punctuate the marinade for these chicken quarters.

    2   frying chickens (3 to 3½ lbs. *each*), quartered
    1   cup dry sherry
    ½   cup salad oil
    1   large onion, finely chopped
    1   tablespoon Worcestershire
    1   teaspoon *each* garlic powder, thyme leaves, oregano leaves, marjoram leaves, dry rosemary, soy sauce, and lemon juice

Reserve chicken necks and giblets for other uses, if desired. Rinse chicken and pat dry. In a large bowl, combine sherry, oil, onion, Worcestershire, garlic powder, thyme, oregano, marjoram, rosemary, soy, and lemon juice. Turn chicken in marinade to coat; then cover and refrigerate for at least 1 hour or until next day, turning occasionally.

About 45 minutes before cooking, start barbecue fire (see "Barbecuing with Direct Heat," page 39). Lift chicken from marinade and drain briefly (reserve marinade). Place chicken, skin side up, on grill 4 to 6 inches above a solid bed of low-glowing coals. Cook, turning and basting occasionally with marinade, until meat near thighbone is no longer pink when slashed (40 to 50 minutes). Makes 8 servings.

Chicken with Brandy Baste

Chicken and fruit are always good together—and here, a brandy baste makes the partnership perfect.

    2   frying chickens (3 to 3½ lbs. *each*), quartered
        Pepper
    ½   cup (¼ lb.) butter or margarine, melted
    ¼   cup *each* firmly packed brown sugar, lemon juice, and brandy
    6   apricots, halved and pitted (or 12 canned apricot halves, drained)
    1   cup pitted fresh dark sweet cherries (or canned pitted dark sweet cherries, drained)

About 45 minutes before cooking, start barbecue fire (see "Barbecuing with Direct Heat," page 39).

Reserve chicken necks and giblets for other uses, if desired. Rinse chicken and pat dry. Sprinkle with pepper. In a bowl, combine butter, sugar, lemon juice, and brandy; turn chicken in butter mixture to coat, then lift out and drain briefly (reserve butter mixture).

Place chicken, skin side up, on grill 4 to 6 inches above a solid bed of low-glowing coals. Cover barbecue, adjust dampers, and cook, turning and basting occasionally with butter mixture, until meat near thighbone is no longer pink when slashed (about 40 minutes).

Meanwhile, arrange apricots (cut side up) and cherries in 2 separate shallow metal pans. Brush fruit with butter mixture, then heat on grill beside chicken for last 5 to 10 minutes of cooking.

To serve, place chicken on a platter and surround with apricots; pour cherries over top. Makes 8 servings.

A Trio of Bastes

For barbecued chicken with minimum fuss and maximum flavor, a quick-to-fix baste is just the thing. Each of the three options below makes enough baste for a cut-up 3 to 3½-pound frying chicken. To barbecue, follow directions for grilling over low-glowing coals (see "Barbecuing with Direct Heat," page 39), placing chicken on grill 4 to 6 inches above coals. Chicken quarters and dark meat pieces will cook in 40 to 50 minutes; breast pieces take about 30 minutes.

Basic Barbecue Sauce

Familiar flavors sometimes please us the most. Tart-sweet, tomatoey barbecue sauce is one such classic. As it cooks, it forms a glaze with a slightly caramelized taste.

- 1 tablespoon salad oil
- ¼ cup finely chopped onion
- 1 can (8 oz.) tomato sauce
- 2½ tablespoons *each* firmly packed brown sugar and red wine vinegar
- 4 teaspoons Worcestershire
- ¼ to ½ teaspoon cracked pepper

Heat oil in a 1 to 2-quart pan over medium heat. Add onion and cook, stirring, until soft. Stir in tomato sauce, sugar, vinegar, Worcestershire, and pepper. Bring to a boil; then reduce heat and simmer, uncovered, until thickened (about 25 minutes). Use to baste chicken during last 20 to 30 minutes of barbecuing.

Buttery Barbecue Sauce

Despite a double dose of heat-producing ingredients, this baste gives cooked birds only a hint of fire. Lemon and vinegar add a pleasant tang; butter keeps the meat moist.

- ½ cup (¼ lb.) butter or margarine
- 1 large clove garlic, minced or pressed
- ¼ cup minced onion
- 3 tablespoons catsup
- 2 tablespoons *each* minced parsley, lemon juice, and wine vinegar
- 1 teaspoon *each* dry mustard and liquid hot pepper seasoning
- ⅛ teaspoon ground red pepper (cayenne)
- ¼ cup beer

Melt butter in a 1½ to 2-quart pan over medium heat; add garlic and onion and cook, stirring, until onion is soft. Stir in catsup, parsley, lemon juice, vinegar, mustard, hot pepper seasoning, pepper, and beer. Bring to a boil; then reduce heat and simmer, uncovered, until flavors are blended (about 5 minutes). Use to baste chicken during last 30 minutes of barbecuing.

Green Onion Butter

Melt some butter, add minced green onions and a sprinkling of seasonings, and you have a simple, savory blend for dressing up grilled chicken pieces. Try it on whole birds, too, such as Chicken with Spinach-Rice Stuffing (page 36).

- ½ cup (¼ lb.) butter or margarine
- 1½ tablespoons *each* finely chopped parsley and minced green onion (including top)
- ½ teaspoon *each* dry mustard and fines herbes
- ⅛ teaspoon *each* garlic powder and liquid hot pepper seasoning
- Dash of pepper

In a small pan, melt butter. Remove from heat; stir in parsley, onion, mustard, fines herbes, garlic powder, hot pepper seasoning, and pepper. Use to baste chicken throughout cooking.

Grilled Asian Chicken

A pungent paste of garlic, cilantro, and crushed peppercorns seasons this bird. You rub the paste into the chicken, then refrigerate it for several hours to allow flavors to penetrate the meat.

2 **whole chicken breasts** (about 1 lb. *each*), split; or 8 **chicken thighs** (about 2½ lbs. *total*)
6 cloves **garlic**
½ cup fresh **cilantro** (coriander) leaves
2 teaspoons whole black **peppercorns**
2 teaspoons **soy sauce**
1 teaspoon **sugar**
5 tablespoons **salad oil**
1 tablespoon **wine vinegar**

Rinse chicken, pat dry, and set aside.

In a blender or food processor, whirl garlic, cilantro, and peppercorns until finely chopped; add soy, sugar, and 4 tablespoons of the salad oil and whirl until a paste forms. Measure out 1½ tablespoons of the paste; cover and refrigerate. Rub remaining paste evenly all over chicken, slipping some under skin. Cover and refrigerate for at least 4 hours or until next day.

About 40 minutes before cooking, start barbecue fire (see "Barbecuing with Direct Heat," page 39). Place chicken, skin side up, on grill 4 to 6 inches above a solid bed of medium-glowing coals. Cook, turning occasionally, until meat near bone is no longer pink when slashed (20 to 25 minutes for breasts, 30 to 40 minutes for thighs). Mix reserved paste with vinegar and remaining 1 tablespoon oil; spoon over chicken. Makes 4 servings.

Bangkok-style Barbecued Birds

With Southeast Asian restaurants springing up all over the United States, more and more diners are discovering the region's cuisines. Here, we present an authoritatively seasoned Thai recipe for eight.

Thai Sauce (recipe follows)
2 **frying chickens** (3 to 3½ lbs. *each*), quartered
½ cup finely chopped fresh **cilantro** (coriander)
⅓ cup coarsely ground **pepper**
24 cloves **garlic**, minced or pressed

Prepare Thai Sauce and set aside. About 40 minutes before cooking, start barbecue fire (see "Barbecuing with Direct Heat," page 39). Reserve chicken necks and giblets for other uses, if desired. Rinse chicken and pat dry. In a bowl, mash together cilantro, pepper, and garlic; rub evenly over chicken.

Place chicken, skin side up, on grill 4 to 6 inches above a solid bed of medium-glowing coals. Cook, turning occasionally, until meat near thighbone is no longer pink when slashed (30 to 40 minutes). Serve with Thai Sauce. Makes 8 servings.

Thai Sauce. In a blender or food processor, whirl until blended: 1 can (8 oz.) **tomato sauce,** 3 tablespoons firmly packed **brown sugar,** 6 cloves **garlic,** ⅛ to ½ teaspoon **ground red pepper** (cayenne), and ¼ cup **cider vinegar.** Add 1¼ cups **golden raisins** and ⅓ cup **water;** whirl until raisins are coarsely chopped. Pour sauce into a 2 to 3-quart pan; bring to a boil over high heat. Boil, stirring, until reduced to 1½ cups (about 10 minutes). If made ahead, let cool; then cover and refrigerate for up to 3 days. Bring to room temperature before serving.

Spanish-style Chicken & Rice

You might call this a barbecue adaptation of Spain's famous *arroz con pollo* ("rice with chicken"). But in the classic dish, the rice is seasoned with saffron; here, it gets its spicy flavor from chorizo sausage.

3 to 3½-pound **frying chicken,** quartered
½ cup (¼ lb.) **butter** or margarine, melted
1 clove **garlic,** minced or pressed
¾ teaspoon **savory** leaves
½ teaspoon **paprika**
¼ teaspoon *each* ground **cinnamon** and dry **tarragon**
Chorizo Rice (recipe follows)

About 45 minutes before cooking, start barbecue fire (see "Barbecuing with Direct Heat," page 39). Reserve chicken neck and giblets for other uses, if desired. Rinse chicken and pat dry.

In a bowl, combine butter, garlic, savory, paprika, cinnamon, and tarragon. Turn chicken in butter mixture to coat, then lift out and drain briefly (reserve butter mixture). Place chicken, skin side up, on grill 4 to 6 inches above a solid bed of low-glowing coals. Cook, turning and basting frequently with butter mixture, until meat near thighbone is no longer pink when slashed (40 to 50 minutes).

Meanwhile, prepare Chorizo Rice, using 1 to 2 tablespoons of the butter mixture. Serve each chicken quarter over rice. Makes 4 servings.

Chorizo Rice. Cut 2 **chorizo sausages** (2½ to 3 oz. *each*) into ½-inch slices. In a wide frying pan over medium heat, cook chorizo until browned on all sides. Add 2 medium-size **onions,** finely chopped; cook, stirring occasionally, until soft. Stir in 3 cups **cooked rice;** 1 cup **frozen peas,** thawed; and 1 **tomato,** peeled and coarsely chopped. Reduce heat to low. Cover and cook, stirring once or twice, until hot throughout (about 10 minutes); then blend in 1 to 2 tablespoons of the **butter mixture.**

Curried Chicken Tortilla Sandwiches

In traditional Indian fashion, chicken is marinated in yogurt and curry spices, then grilled and served with cucumbers and a minty yogurt sauce. In place of the usual *chapaties* (Indian flat bread), we use flour tortillas for wrappers.

   2 **whole chicken breasts (about 1 lb.** *each***), skinned, boned, and split (see page 93)**
   2 **cups plain yogurt**
1½ **teaspoons curry powder**
   ½ **teaspoon** *each* **ground cumin, coriander, and ginger**
       About ½ teaspoon garlic salt
   ¼ to ½ **teaspoon ground red pepper (cayenne)**
   2 **tablespoons lemon juice**
   8 **flour tortillas,** *each* **about 8 inches in diameter**
   2 **tablespoons finely chopped fresh mint**
   8 **small romaine lettuce leaves**
   1 **small cucumber, cut in half lengthwise and thinly sliced**

Rinse chicken, pat dry, and cut into 1-inch chunks. In a bowl, stir together 1 cup of the yogurt, curry powder, cumin, coriander, ginger, ½ teaspoon of the garlic salt, pepper, and lemon juice. Add chicken and stir to coat. Cover and refrigerate for at least 4 hours or until next day, stirring occasionally.

About 45 minutes before cooking, start barbecue fire (see "Barbecuing with Direct Heat," page 39). Lift chicken from marinade, drain briefly (discard marinade), and thread on 4 bamboo or metal skewers. Sprinkle each tortilla with a few drops of water; then stack and wrap in heavy-duty foil.

Place chicken on grill 4 to 6 inches above a solid bed of low-glowing coals. Place tortillas at edge of grill (not directly above coals). Cook, turning chicken and tortillas occasionally, until meat is no longer pink when slashed and tortillas are warm (10 to 12 minutes). Keep warm.

In a bowl, stir together mint and remaining 1 cup yogurt. Season to taste with garlic salt. To eat, place a romaine leaf down center of a tortilla and top with chicken, cucumber, and yogurt sauce; roll up and eat out of hand. Makes 4 servings.

Chicken Wings with Grilled Potatoes

Marinated chicken wings with grilled potatoes are a good choice for a picnic in the park. You can cook them together on a large grill in about 30 minutes.

   4 **pounds (about 20) chicken wings**
   ½ **cup soy sauce**
   1 **clove garlic, minced or pressed**
   1 **teaspoon ground ginger**
   2 **tablespoons** *each* **firmly packed brown sugar, lemon juice, and salad oil**
   ¼ **cup finely chopped onion**
   ¼ **teaspoon pepper**
   4 **large russet potatoes**
       Melted butter or margarine
       Garlic salt

Rinse chicken and pat dry. Bend wings akimbo (see page 65). In a large bowl, combine soy, garlic, ginger, sugar, lemon juice, oil, onion, and pepper. Stir in wings; cover and refrigerate for 2 hours, turning wings several times.

About 40 minutes before cooking, start barbecue fire (see "Barbecuing with Direct Heat," page 39). Meanwhile, scrub potatoes (do not peel). Cut lengthwise into ¼-inch slices; brush generously with butter and sprinkle with garlic salt.

Lift chicken from marinade and drain briefly (discard marinade). For easy turning, arrange chicken in a hinged wire basket and place on grill 4 to 6 inches above a solid bed of medium-glowing coals (or simply place individual wings on grill). Arrange potatoes alongside (not in basket). Cook, turning chicken and potatoes occasionally, until meat near bone is no longer pink when slashed and potatoes are soft when pierced (about 30 minutes). Makes about 4 servings.

Kettle Cookery

Chicken simmered, poached & steamed

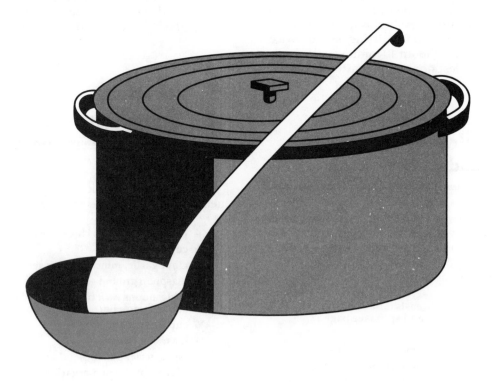

Though "kettle cookery" may bring to mind a steaming cauldron of stew, we've updated the concept to include much more. Soups and stews are still well represented, of course—down-home types as well as fancier creations. But you'll also find a variety of other dishes: curries, a classic cacciatore, pot stickers, and an unusual steamed pot-au-feu. Cooking vessels vary, too, from big pots to steamers to covered frying pans. What ties these recipes together is a similarity in cooking method: all cook gently on top of the range, with broth or other liquid.

Braising is one popular type of kettle cookery—meat is first browned, then simmered in a small amount of liquid. For the tenderest chicken, regulate heat so liquid bubbles gently; boiling may result in overcooking. And for extra-moist breast meat when you cook a cut-up chicken, wait until 15 to 20 minutes before the end of cooking to add breast pieces to the pan.

Poaching and steeping differ from braising in that chicken is completely submerged in liquid. Steeping is an especially gentle technique —the pan is removed from the heat once the chicken is added, so the meat cooks solely by heat retained in the liquid.

Steaming cooks chicken more indirectly than poaching or steeping; the meat is held above simmering liquid and cooked by hot vapors rising from it. The classic tool for steaming is a steamer—a pan with a perforated insert—but you can also achieve excellent results using a wire rack set in a large pan.

North Indian Chicken Curry

Pleasantly spicy but not too hot, this chicken curry features a thick sauce of onions and yogurt. Offer a mixture of pulverized sweet and savory spices, called *garam masala,* to sprinkle atop each serving. In addition to the spices, you might offer a mango or tomato chutney.

    Garam Masala (recipe follows)
  2 medium-size onions, cut into chunks
  2 cloves garlic
  1 to 2 teaspoons minced fresh or canned
    jalapeño pepper (remove seeds for a
    milder curry)
  3 tablespoons coarsely chopped fresh
    ginger
    About ¼ cup water
  ⅓ cup salad oil
  2 tablespoons tomato paste
  1 teaspoon turmeric
  ¼ to ½ teaspoon ground red pepper
    (cayenne)
  ½ cup plain yogurt
  6 whole chicken legs, thighs attached
    (about 3 lbs. *total*)
    Salt
    Fresh cilantro (coriander) sprigs

Prepare Garam Masala; set aside. In a blender or food processor, whirl onions, garlic, jalapeño pepper, ginger, and ¼ cup of the water until puréed. Pour into a wide frying pan and cook over medium heat, stirring occasionally, until dry and thick (15 to 20 minutes). Reduce heat to medium-low; stir in oil, tomato paste, turmeric, red pepper, and yogurt. Cook, uncovered, stirring occasionally, until thickened (5 to 10 more minutes).

Meanwhile, rinse chicken and pat dry. Add to sauce and turn to coat. Cover and simmer, turning once, until meat near thighbone is no longer pink when slashed (40 to 45 minutes); add about 1 tablespoon more water if sauce begins to stick to pan. Transfer chicken to a serving dish. Skim and discard fat from sauce, then season to taste with salt. Spoon sauce over chicken. Garnish with cilantro. Pass Garam Masala at the table to sprinkle over each serving. Makes 6 servings.

Garam Masala. In a small frying pan over medium-low heat, cook 3 tablespoons **coriander seeds** and 2 teaspoons **cumin seeds** until lightly browned (about 4 minutes), shaking pan often. Place in a blender, then add 8 **whole cloves;** 1 **cinnamon stick** (about 2 inches long), broken in half; ½ teaspoon **whole black peppercorns;** and 4 **bay leaves.** Whirl until finely ground. Store airtight.

Lime Chicken

Boned chicken breasts with a tangy, creamy sauce are a good choice for a company meal. If you have the chicken boned at the market, be sure to ask for the trimmings; you'll need them to make the broth that flavors the herb and mushroom sauce.

  4 whole chicken breasts (about
    1 lb. *each*)
    Cooking Broth (recipe follows)
  2 tablespoons butter or margarine
  2 tablespoons salad oil
  1 medium-size onion, sliced
  ½ pound mushrooms, sliced
  3 tablespoons all-purpose flour
  ½ cup dry vermouth
  3 tablespoons lime juice
  1 bay leaf
  ¼ teaspoon *each* oregano, thyme, and
    marjoram leaves
  ¼ teaspoon dry basil
  ¼ cup whipping cream
    Salt and pepper
    Chopped parsley

Skin, bone, and split chicken breasts (see page 93), reserving trimmings for Cooking Broth. Rinse chicken and pat dry; then set aside. Prepare broth; set aside.

Melt butter in oil in a wide frying pan over medium heat. Add chicken, a portion at a time, without crowding; cook, turning once, until browned on both sides. Lift out and set aside.

Add onion and mushrooms to pan; cook, stirring, until onion is soft. Stir in flour and cook until bubbly; then add vermouth, lime juice, broth, bay leaf, oregano, thyme, marjoram, and basil. Cook, stirring, until sauce is bubbly and thickened. Stir in cream, then return chicken to pan. Cover and simmer, turning once, until meat is no longer pink when slashed in thickest part (about 15 minutes).

Lift chicken from sauce and transfer to a platter. Skim and discard fat from sauce; season to taste with salt and pepper. Spoon a little of the sauce over chicken; garnish with parsley. Pass remaining sauce at the table. Makes 8 servings.

Cooking Broth. In a 2 to 3-quart pan, combine reserved **trimmings from chicken breasts;** 1 small **carrot,** chopped; 1 stalk **celery,** chopped; and 1⅓ cups **regular-strength chicken broth,** homemade (page 53) or purchased. Bring to a boil over high heat; then reduce heat, cover, and simmer for 45 minutes. Strain broth; discard bones, skin, and vegetables.

Sesame Chicken Pot Stickers

Pot stickers are delightful fare for a party or light meal. (You'll find the wrappers in Asian markets and well-stocked supermarkets.)

- 2 small whole chicken breasts (¾ lb. *each*), skinned, boned, and split (see page 93)
- ¼ cup sesame oil
- 1 cup finely chopped celery
- ½ cup chopped green onions (including tops)
- 3 tablespoons dry sherry
- 2 tablespoons cornstarch
- 1 teaspoon sugar
- ½ teaspoon salt
- 1 package (10 oz.) pot sticker wrappers (*gyoza*) or won ton skins
- 4 tablespoons salad oil
- 1 cup water
  Distilled white vinegar, soy sauce, and chili oil

Rinse chicken, pat dry, and finely chop. Place in a bowl and stir in sesame oil, celery, onions, sherry, cornstarch, sugar, and salt.

Set out 6 to 8 wrappers at a time; keep others tightly covered. Place 2 teaspoons of the filling in center of each wrapper; moisten edges with water, fold in half over filling, and pinch edges to seal. Set on a baking sheet, seam side up; keep covered until all wrappers have been filled. (At this point, you may freeze pot stickers on baking sheets, then transfer to heavy plastic bags and freeze for up to 3 months. Do not thaw before cooking.)

Heat 1 tablespoon of the salad oil in a wide frying pan over medium heat. Add 12 pot stickers, seam side up. Cook, uncovered, until bottoms are deep golden brown (5 to 7 minutes). Pour in ¼ cup of the water; at once reduce heat to low, cover, and cook for 6 more minutes. Remove from pan and keep warm. Repeat with remaining salad oil, pot stickers, and water.

Provide diners with vinegar, soy, and chili oil to make dipping sauce (suggest 1 tablespoon vinegar mixed with ½ teaspoon soy and a dash of chili oil). Makes about 4 dozen (8 to 12 appetizer servings or 6 main-dish servings).

Chicken Caper

Chicken cooked in apple juice with rum and capers has a sweet-sour flavor with caramel overtones.

- 3½ to 4-pound frying chicken, cut up
  All-purpose flour
  Pepper and ground ginger
- ¼ cup butter or margarine
- 1 large onion, chopped
- 1 clove garlic, minced or pressed
- 1 can (12 oz.) frozen apple juice concentrate, thawed (do not dilute)
- 3 tablespoons *each* lemon juice, dark rum, and drained capers

Reserve chicken neck and giblets for other uses, if desired. Rinse chicken and pat dry. Dust with flour; shake off excess. Sprinkle lightly on all sides with pepper and ginger.

Melt butter in a wide frying pan over medium heat. Add chicken, a portion at a time, without crowding; cook, turning, until browned on all sides. Lift out and set aside.

Add onion and garlic to pan and cook, stirring, until onion is soft. Stir in apple juice, lemon juice, rum, and capers. Return chicken to pan. Increase heat to high and bring juice mixture to a boil; then reduce heat, cover, and simmer, turning once, until meat near thighbone is no longer pink when slashed (35 to 40 minutes).

Transfer chicken to a platter and keep warm. Skim and discard fat from pan juices; if necessary, boil juices, uncovered, until slightly thickened. Pour sauce into a bowl and offer to spoon over individual portions. Makes 4 or 5 servings.

Classic Chicken Cacciatore

Pollo alla cacciatora—"chicken hunter style"—is an Italian classic, savory with red wine and herbs.

- 3 to 3½-pound frying chicken, cut up
- 2 tablespoons butter or margarine
- 2 tablespoons olive oil or salad oil
- 1 medium-size onion, chopped
- 1 clove garlic, minced or pressed
- 1 large stalk celery, finely chopped
- 1 medium-size carrot, shredded
- ¼ pound medium-size mushrooms, quartered
- 1 can (16 oz.) tomatoes
- ⅓ cup dry red wine
- ⅓ cup chopped parsley
- ½ teaspoon dry rosemary
- ¼ teaspoon *each* dry basil and oregano leaves
  Salt and pepper

Reserve chicken neck and giblets for other uses, if desired. Rinse chicken and pat dry. Melt butter in oil in a wide frying pan over medium-high heat. Add chicken, a portion at a time, without crowding; cook, turning, until browned on all sides. Lift out and set aside. Discard all but 3 tablespoons drippings.

Add onion, garlic, celery, carrot, and mushrooms to pan. Cook, stirring occasionally, until onion is soft. Return chicken to pan; stir in tomatoes (break up with a spoon) and their liquid, wine, ¼ cup of the parsley, rosemary, basil, and oregano. Bring to a boil; reduce heat, cover, and simmer, turning once, until meat near thighbone is no longer pink when slashed (35 to 40 minutes). Transfer chicken to a platter and keep warm.

Skim and discard fat from sauce; season to taste with salt and pepper. Increase heat to high and boil, stirring, until slightly thickened. Spoon over chicken and sprinkle with remaining parsley. Makes about 4 servings.

Garlic Celebration Chicken

No matter what the occasion, a garlicky chicken dish like this one is cause enough for celebration.

> 3 to 3½-pound frying chicken, cut up
> 4 slices bacon
> 2 medium-size onions, chopped
> 5 cloves garlic, minced or pressed
> 1 cup dry white wine
> ¼ cup dry vermouth or dry white wine
> 1 tablespoon dry basil
> 1 teaspoon poultry seasoning
> Hot buttered noodles
> Salt and pepper
> 1 tablespoon *each* cornstarch and water
> 2 medium-size tomatoes, cut into wedges

Reserve chicken neck and giblets for other uses, if desired. Rinse chicken, pat dry, and set aside.

In a wide frying pan, cook bacon over medium heat until crisp. Lift out, leaving drippings in pan; drain, crumble, and set aside.

Increase heat to medium-high. Add chicken to pan, a portion at a time, without crowding; cook, turning, until browned on all sides. Lift out and set aside.

Add onions and garlic to pan and cook, stirring, until onions are soft. Spoon off and discard any fat from pan; add wine, vermouth, basil, poultry seasoning, bacon, and chicken. Bring to a boil

over high heat; then reduce heat, cover, and simmer until meat near thighbone is no longer pink when slashed (35 to 40 minutes).

Arrange chicken and noodles on a platter; keep warm. Skim and discard fat from pan juices, then season to taste with salt and pepper. Combine cornstarch and water, stir into pan juices, and cook, stirring, until thickened. Garnish chicken with tomatoes; pass sauce at the table. Makes about 4 servings.

Indian Pan-roasted Chicken

How do you cook a whole chicken? Roasting isn't the only answer—this spice-fragrant bird is braised.

> 3 to 3½-pound whole frying chicken
> Pepper
> Seasoned Broth (recipe follows)
> 3 tablespoons salad oil
> 2 bay leaves
> 1 cinnamon stick (about 3 inches long)
> 6 whole cloves
> 5 whole black peppercorns
> 3 cloves garlic, minced or pressed
> Orange slices
> Fresh cilantro (coriander) sprigs

Remove chicken neck and giblets; reserve for other uses, if desired. Then remove and discard skin and lumps of fat. Rinse chicken inside and out, pat dry, and sprinkle lightly with pepper. Tie ends of drumsticks together. Prepare Seasoned Broth; set aside.

Heat oil in a wok or 5 to 6-quart pan over medium heat. Add bay leaves, cinnamon stick, cloves, and peppercorns; then add chicken and cook, uncovered, turning occasionally, until browned on all sides (about 20 minutes). Stir in Seasoned Broth and garlic. Bring to a boil; reduce heat, cover, and simmer until meat near thighbone is no longer pink when slashed (20 to 25 more minutes), turning chicken occasionally.

Transfer chicken to a serving dish. Skim and discard any fat from pan juices; pour over chicken. Garnish with orange slices and cilantro. Makes about 4 servings.

Seasoned Broth. In a bowl, combine 1 cup **regular-strength chicken broth,** homemade (page 53) or purchased; 2 teaspoons *each* **soy sauce** and **Worcestershire;** 1 teaspoon **ground cumin;** ¼ teaspoon **ground red pepper** (cayenne); and ⅛ teaspoon **ground cardamom.**

Cuban Chicken

Raisins and olives in a spicy tomato sauce give a Cuban accent to chicken.

      3 to 3½-pound frying chicken, cut up
  2 tablespoons olive oil or salad oil
  2 cloves garlic, minced or pressed
  1 large onion, chopped
  1 large green bell pepper, seeded and
       chopped
  4 small thin-skinned potatoes
  ¾ teaspoon *each* oregano leaves and
       ground cumin
  1 large can (15 oz.) tomato sauce
  ⅓ cup dry white wine or water
  ½ cup *each* raisins and pitted ripe olives
  1 cup frozen peas, thawed

Reserve chicken neck and giblets for other uses, if desired. Rinse chicken; pat dry. Heat oil in a 5 to 6-quart pan over medium-high heat. Add chicken, a portion at a time, without crowding; cook, turning, until browned on all sides. Lift out and set aside. Discard all but 2 tablespoons drippings.

Add garlic, onion, and bell pepper to pan. Cook, stirring, until onion is soft. Cut potatoes into 1-inch chunks; add to pan along with oregano, cumin, tomato sauce, wine, raisins, olives, and chicken. Bring to a boil; then reduce heat, cover, and simmer, turning chicken once, until meat near thighbone is no longer pink when slashed (35 to 40 minutes). Skim and discard fat from sauce. Stir in peas; cook just until hot. Makes about 4 servings.

Chicken Breasts Véronique

As *Véronique* suggests, this handsome presentation of chicken breasts features green grapes.

  4 whole chicken breasts (about 1 lb. *each*),
       skinned, boned, and split (see page 93)
  2 tablespoons butter or margarine
  1½ tablespoons orange marmalade
  ½ teaspoon dry tarragon
  ½ cup dry white wine
  ½ cup whipping cream
       Salt
  1½ cups seedless green grapes

Rinse chicken and pat dry. Melt butter in a wide frying pan over medium heat. Add chicken,

a portion at a time, without crowding; cook, turning once, until lightly browned on both sides.

Stir in marmalade, tarragon, and wine. Bring to a boil over high heat; then reduce heat, cover, and simmer, turning once, until meat is no longer pink when slashed in thickest part (about 15 minutes). Transfer chicken to a serving dish; keep warm. Add cream to pan juices; boil, stirring, until slightly reduced. Season to taste with salt, then mix in grapes and return to a boil. Pour over chicken. Makes 8 servings.

Coq au Vin

(Pictured on facing page)

This classic French dish gets its robust flavor from red wine and Dijon mustard.

      3 to 3½-pound frying chicken, cut up
  ⅓ pound pork shoulder steak (blade
       steak), boned and cut into ½-inch cubes
  8 small white boiling onions
  ½ pound small mushrooms
  1¾ cups regular-strength chicken broth,
       homemade (page 53) or purchased
       (one 14½-oz. can)
  1 cup dry red wine
  2 tablespoons Dijon mustard
  1 teaspoon *each* cornstarch and water
  2 tablespoons chopped parsley

Reserve chicken neck and giblets for other uses, if desired. Rinse chicken, pat dry, and set aside.

In a wide frying pan over medium-high heat, cook pork, stirring, until crisp and well browned. Lift out and set aside, leaving drippings in pan.

Add chicken to pan, a portion at a time, without crowding; cook, turning, until browned on all sides. Lift out and set aside. Add onions to pan; cook, stirring, until browned on all sides. Add mushrooms; cook, stirring occasionally, until liquid has evaporated. Set onions and mushrooms aside.

Pour broth into pan, increase heat to high, and boil until reduced to 1 cup, stirring to scrape browned bits free. Stir in wine and mustard; return chicken, onions, and mushrooms to pan. Bring to a boil; then reduce heat, cover, and simmer until meat near thighbone is no longer pink when slashed (35 to 40 minutes). Stir in pork; return to a simmer. Skim and discard fat from sauce.

Transfer chicken and vegetables to a serving dish. Combine cornstarch and water; stir into sauce. Bring to a boil, stirring; pour over chicken. Sprinkle with parsley. Makes about 4 servings.

You don't have to be French to enjoy hearty Coq au Vin (facing page). Cooks and diners the world around appreciate the robust red wine flavor and rich color of this simmered chicken dish.

Chicken Couscous

"Couscous" has two meanings. It's a traditional North African stew of meat and vegetables; it's also the name of the semolina wheat served with the stew. (You'll find the grain in Middle Eastern groceries and well-stocked supermarkets.)

   Savory Stew Broth (recipe follows)
   Hot Tomato Sauce (recipe follows)
2 tablespoons olive oil or salad oil
   Chicken breasts, drumsticks, and thighs (reserved from Savory Stew Broth)
5 medium-size carrots, cut into halves crosswise
1 small head cabbage, cut into wedges
2 cans (16 oz. *each*) garbanzo beans
1 pound *each* crookneck squash and zucchini (ends trimmed), cut into halves lengthwise
   Steamed Couscous Grain (recipe follows)

Up to 2 days ahead, prepare stew broth; also prepare tomato sauce, using 2 cups of the broth.

Heat oil in an 8 to 10-quart pan over medium-high heat. Add chicken to pan, a portion at a time, without crowding; cook, turning, until browned on all sides. Discard pan drippings.

Return chicken to pan with carrots, cabbage, and remaining stew broth. Bring to a boil over high heat; reduce heat, cover, and simmer for 10 minutes. Add garbanzos and their liquid, crookneck squash, and zucchini. Cover and continue to simmer until meat near thighbone is no longer pink when slashed (25 to 30 more minutes).

Meanwhile, prepare Steamed Couscous Grain and reheat tomato sauce. Transfer chicken and vegetables (except garbanzos) to a rimmed platter; keep warm. With a slotted spoon, transfer garbanzos to a serving bowl; keep warm. Pour broth into a pitcher. To serve, spoon grain into individual bowls; top with chicken, vegetables, and garbanzos. Pass broth and tomato sauce to pour over individual servings. Makes about 10 servings.

Savory Stew Broth. Rinse and pat dry 2 **frying chickens** (3½ to 4 lbs. *each*), cut up. Set breasts, drumsticks, and thighs aside for use in stew; also reserve liver for other uses, if desired. Place remaining giblets, necks, backs, and wings in a 6 to 8-quart pan. Then add 2 large **onions,** sliced; 1 large **carrot,** cut into chunks; 1 **green bell pepper,** seeded and cut into chunks; 1 **turnip,** cut into chunks; 6 tablespoons **tomato paste;** 1½ tablespoons **paprika;** ½ teaspoon *each* **ground cinnamon** and **pepper;** and 7 cups **water.** Bring to a boil over high heat; reduce heat, cover, and simmer for 2 hours. Strain;

discard chicken and vegetables. (At this point, you may let cool, then cover and refrigerate for up to 2 days.) Skim (or lift off) and discard fat from broth.

Hot Tomato Sauce. In a 2 to 3-quart pan, combine 2 cups **Savory Stew Broth;** 15 ounces (one 12-oz. can plus 6 tablespoons) **tomato paste;** 2 tablespoons **olive oil** or salad oil; 3 cloves **garlic,** minced or pressed; ¾ teaspoon **ground cumin;** and 4 teaspoons *each* **ground red pepper** (cayenne) and **sugar.** Bring to a boil over medium-high heat; reduce heat and cook, stirring, until thickened (5 minutes). Season to taste with **salt.** If made ahead, let cool; cover and refrigerate for up to 2 days.

Steamed Couscous Grain. In a 3 to 4-quart pan, combine 3 cups **water,** ½ cup (¼ lb.) **butter** or margarine, ½ cup **raisins,** 1 teaspoon **salt,** and ½ teaspoon **ground cinnamon.** Bring to a boil over high heat; add 1 package (1 lb.) **quick-cooking couscous.** Cover, remove from heat, and let stand until liquid has been absorbed (about 5 minutes). With a fork or a slotted spoon, toss couscous until light, fluffy, and free of lumps.

Chicken Soup with Matzo Balls

A traditional opening to a Passover meal, matzo ball soup is good-tasting food any time of year.

3   eggs
    About ⅓ cup chopped parsley
3   tablespoons water
2   tablespoons finely chopped onion
3   tablespoons chicken fat or solid vegetable shortening, melted and cooled
1¼ teaspoons salt
⅛   teaspoon *each* ground nutmeg and pepper
¾   cup matzo meal
6   cups regular-strength chicken broth, homemade (next page) or purchased (one 49½-oz. can)
2   medium-size carrots, thinly sliced

In a bowl, lightly beat eggs; then stir in 3 tablespoons of the parsley, water, onion, chicken fat, salt, nutmeg, and pepper. Add matzo meal and stir until blended. Cover and refrigerate for 30 minutes. Shape rounded tablespoonfuls of matzo mixture (it will be slightly sticky) into balls.

In a 2 to 3-quart pan, bring broth to a boil over high heat. Add carrots and matzo balls, reduce heat, cover, and simmer until matzo balls are firm to the touch and a wooden pick inserted in center comes out clean (about 35 minutes). Sprinkle with remaining parsley. Makes 6 first-course servings.

Chicken & Dumplings

Tender stewed chicken topped with fluffy dumplings—it's an old-fashioned favorite, so good it never goes out of style. For best results, cook the dumplings without peeking until it's time to check for doneness.

> 3 to 3½-pound frying chicken, cut up
> 2 tablespoons salad oil
> 1 large onion, sliced
> 6 medium-size carrots, cut into 1½-inch lengths
> 1½ teaspoons rubbed sage
> 4 cups regular-strength chicken broth, homemade (this page) or purchased (about two 14½-oz. cans)
> ⅓ cup dry white wine
> Salt and pepper
> Poppy Seed Dumplings (recipe follows)
> Chopped parsley

Reserve chicken neck and giblets for other uses, if desired. Rinse chicken and pat dry. Heat oil in a 5 to 6-quart pan over medium-high heat. Add chicken, a portion at a time, without crowding; cook, turning, until browned on all sides. Lift out and set aside.

Reduce heat to medium. Add onion to pan and cook, stirring, until soft. Add carrots, sage, broth, wine, and chicken. Increase heat to high and bring mixture to a boil; then reduce heat, cover, and simmer for 20 minutes. Skim and discard fat. Season to taste with salt and pepper.

Prepare Poppy Seed Dumplings; drop onto chicken, spacing slightly apart. Cover and cook until dumplings are firm to the touch and a wooden pick inserted in center comes out clean (20 to 25 minutes). Garnish with parsley and serve immediately. Makes about 6 servings.

Poppy Seed Dumplings. In a bowl, sift together 2 cups **all-purpose flour,** 4 teaspoons **baking powder,** and ½ teaspoon **salt.** Stir in 1 tablespoon **poppy seeds.** Using a pastry blender or 2 knives, cut in 5 tablespoons firm **butter** or margarine until mixture resembles coarse meal. Make a well in center; pour in 1 cup **milk** all at once and stir with a fork until dough cleans sides of bowl. Form dough into 6 equal balls.

Homemade Chicken Broth

Though canned chicken broth is excellent, making broth from scratch is easy and economical—and it takes only a few hours. Your kitchen will smell marvelous while the broth simmers; and when it's done, you'll have a richly flavored base for soups, sauces, gravies, and stews.

One obvious economy of cutting up a chicken at home is that nothing need go to waste. For our broth, save wings, backs, necks, and even the bones and skins from boned chicken breasts. Collect and store them in the freezer until you have 5 pounds.

Homemade broth freezes beautifully. Let it cool after cooking, then store it in containers that hold enough for a full recipe of soup or stew. Or freeze it in ice cube trays; then release the cubes and store them in freezer bags, ready to use whenever you need a small amount of broth.

> 5 pounds chicken backs, necks, wings, and trimmings (skin and bones leftover from boning)
> 3 quarts water
> 2 carrots, cut into chunks
> 2 medium-size onions, quartered
> 2 stalks celery, cut into pieces
> 1 bay leaf
> 6 whole black peppercorns
> ¼ teaspoon thyme leaves

Place chicken, water, carrots, onions, celery, bay leaf, peppercorns, and thyme in a 6 to 8-quart pan. Bring to a boil over high heat; then reduce heat, cover, and simmer until meat falls from bones (about 2½ hours). Let cool.

Strain broth; discard chicken, vegetables, and seasonings. Cover and refrigerate for up to 4 days; lift off and discard solidified fat before using.

To freeze, transfer broth (skimmed of fat) to freezer containers, leaving ½ to 1 inch head space. Cover and freeze for up to 6 months. Makes about 3 quarts.

A **whole garden full of produce** goes into the pot to make Spring Harvest
Chicken Soup (facing page). For a special finish, small toast rounds
spread with herb mayonnaise accompany individual servings.

Spring Harvest Chicken Soup

(Pictured on facing page)

Spring vegetables—peas, green beans, asparagus, and more—give this soup its fresh flavor.

        Herb Mayonnaise (recipe follows)
        3 to 3½-pound frying chicken, cut up
    2   cups regular-strength chicken broth,
        homemade (page 53) or purchased
        (about one 14½-oz. can)
    8   cups water
    1   large onion, cut into chunks
    1   clove garlic, cut in half
        Toast Rounds (recipe follows)
    ½   pound asparagus, tough ends removed
    2   large leeks (about 1 lb. *total*)
    ¼   pound green beans, ends removed
    ½   pound peas in the pod, shelled
    ¼   pound mushrooms, sliced
        Salt and pepper

Prepare Herb Mayonnaise; cover and refrigerate.

Reserve chicken neck and giblets for other uses, if desired. Rinse chicken, pat dry, and place in a 6 to 8-quart pan; add broth, water, onion, and garlic. Bring to a boil over high heat; then reduce heat, cover, and simmer until meat near thighbone is no longer pink when slashed (40 to 45 minutes).

Lift out chicken and let cool; meanwhile, prepare Toast Rounds and set aside. Remove chicken skin and bones and return to pan; cut meat into bite-size pieces and set aside. Cover pan and simmer broth for 30 more minutes.

Cut off asparagus tips and set aside; then cut stalks into 1-inch pieces. Trim and discard ends and tops from leeks, leaving about 3 inches of green leaves. Discard tough outer leaves. Split leeks lengthwise; rinse well, then thinly slice crosswise. Cut beans into 1-inch pieces.

Strain broth and discard bones, skin, and vegetables. Return broth to pan and bring to a simmer. Add asparagus tips and stalks, leeks, beans, peas, and mushrooms; simmer, uncovered, until beans are tender-crisp to bite (5 to 7 minutes). Add chicken and continue to simmer until heated through. Season to taste with salt and pepper.

Spread Toast Rounds with Herb Mayonnaise; pass at the table. Makes 6 to 8 servings.

Herb Mayonnaise. Combine 1 cup **mayonnaise**, 1 clove **garlic**, minced or pressed, and 2 teaspoons chopped **fresh herbs** such as rosemary, oregano, basil, thyme, and marjoram (or 1 teaspoon *total* dry herbs). Cover; refrigerate for at least 2 hours.

Toast Rounds. Thinly slice 1 **slender baguette** (8 oz.); arrange slices in a single layer on baking sheets. Bake in a 350° oven until golden (about 15 minutes); let cool.

Colombian Chicken & Potato Soup

Almost every version of Colombian *ajiaco* uses chicken and potatoes; our rendition of this soup also includes carrots and slices of corn on the cob.

        3½ to 4-pound frying chicken, cut up
    3   quarts regular-strength chicken broth,
        homemade (page 53) or purchased
        (two 49½-oz. cans)
    2   large russet potatoes, cut into 1-inch
        chunks
    2   large onions, finely chopped
    2   cloves garlic, minced or pressed
    ½   teaspoon thyme leaves
    ¾   teaspoon ground cumin
    1   pound medium-size red thin-skinned
        potatoes
    3   large carrots, cut into ¼-inch-thick slices
    1   bay leaf
    3   ears corn, cut into 1-inch lengths
    2   firm-ripe avocados
        Lime wedges
    1   cup chopped fresh cilantro (coriander)
    ½   cup thinly sliced green onions
        (including tops)
    ⅓   cup drained capers
    1   cup whipping cream

Reserve chicken neck and giblets for other uses, if desired. Rinse chicken, pat dry, and place in an 8 to 10-quart pan; add broth, russet potatoes, chopped onions, garlic, thyme, and cumin. Bring to a boil over high heat; then reduce heat, cover, and simmer for 20 minutes.

Cut thin-skinned potatoes into halves; add to pan with carrots and bay leaf. Cover and continue to simmer until meat near thighbone is no longer pink when slashed (20 to 25 more minutes). Skim and discard fat from broth. Add corn; cover and simmer until corn is hot (about 5 more minutes). Meanwhile, pit, peel, and quarter avocados.

Ladle broth, chicken, and vegetables into wide soup bowls. Pass lime wedges to squeeze into soup; offer avocados, cilantro, green onions, capers, and cream to add to individual portions. Eat with knife and fork. Makes 6 to 8 servings.

Chicken Peanut Stew

In its homeland, this West African dish is flavored with peanuts ground to a paste, but we've substituted peanut butter for convenience. Traditional accompaniments include rice and cooked fresh spinach; prepare them while the stew simmers.

> 4 *each* chicken drumsticks and thighs (about 2 lbs. *total*)
> 2 tablespoons salad oil
> 2 medium-size onions, chopped
> 2 medium-size tomatoes, peeled and chopped
> 2 cups regular-strength chicken broth, homemade (page 53) or purchased (about one 14½-oz. can)
> ½ teaspoon liquid hot pepper seasoning
> 1 tablespoon lime juice
> ¼ teaspoon ground nutmeg
> ⅛ teaspoon ground cloves
> 1 cinnamon stick (about 2 inches long)
> 5 carrots, cut diagonally into 3-inch pieces
> 2 green bell peppers, seeded and chopped
> ½ cup creamy peanut butter
> 2 tablespoons cornstarch
> Accompaniments (suggestions follow)

Rinse chicken and pat dry. Heat oil in a 5 to 6-quart pan over medium-high heat. Add chicken, a portion at a time, without crowding; cook, turning, until browned on all sides. Lift out and set aside. Discard all but 2 tablespoons drippings.

Add onions to pan; reduce heat to medium and cook, stirring, until soft. Add tomatoes, 1½ cups of the broth, hot pepper seasoning, lime juice, nutmeg, cloves, cinnamon stick, carrots, and chicken.

Bring to a boil; then reduce heat, cover, and simmer for 20 minutes. Add bell peppers; cover and continue to simmer until meat near thighbone is no longer pink when slashed (15 to 20 more minutes). Skim and discard fat from sauce.

In a bowl, blend peanut butter with cornstarch; then stir in remaining broth until mixture is smooth. Pour into stew. Cook, stirring, until sauce is thickened (about 5 minutes). Serve with accompaniments as directed below. Makes about 4 servings.

Accompaniments. You'll need 4 cups hot **cooked rice**, 2 to 3 cups hot **cooked spinach**, ½ cup chopped **green onions** (including tops), and 1 cup *each* **roasted salted peanuts** and **unsweetened shredded coconut.** Spoon rice into wide soup bowls or rimmed plates; top with spinach, stew, onions, peanuts, and coconut.

Chicken Gumbo

Not all gumbos contain okra or filé powder for body, but most are thickened by a flour-fat mixture called a *roux*. Making a roux usually involves slow cooking on the range, with constant stirring—but here, the roux cooks almost unattended in a hot oven.

> 3 to 3½-pound frying chicken, cut up
> 1 pound andouille or linguisa sausage, sliced ½ inch thick
> Salad oil
> ¾ cup all-purpose flour
> 2 large onions, chopped
> 1 large green bell pepper, seeded and thinly sliced
> 4 stalks celery, sliced
> 2 cloves garlic, minced or pressed
> 1 can (16 oz.) tomatoes
> ¼ teaspoon black pepper
> ¼ to ½ teaspoon crushed red pepper
> 6 cups regular-strength chicken broth, homemade (page 53) or purchased (one 49½-oz. can)
> ¾ pound okra, ends trimmed; or 1 package (10 oz.) frozen whole okra, thawed
> ½ cup finely chopped parsley
> Hot cooked rice
> Gumbo filé

Reserve chicken neck and giblets for other uses, if desired. Rinse chicken, pat dry, and set aside.

In a wide, heavy ovenproof frying pan, cook sausage over medium-high heat until browned. Lift out and set aside, leaving drippings in pan. Add chicken, a portion at a time, without crowding; cook, turning, until browned on all sides. Lift out and set aside.

Remove pan from heat. Measure drippings and add enough oil to make ¾ cup; return to pan. Stir in flour until smooth. Place pan, uncovered, in a 400° oven; bake until roux is dark brown (about 35 minutes), stirring thoroughly every 15 minutes.

Remove pan from oven. Scrape roux into a 5 to 6-quart pan. Add onions, bell pepper, celery, and garlic; cook over medium heat, stirring frequently, until vegetables are soft (15 to 20 minutes). Stir in tomatoes (break up with a spoon) and their liquid, black pepper, red pepper, broth, chicken, and sausage. Bring to a boil; reduce heat, cover, and simmer for 30 minutes. (At this point, you may let cool, then cover and refrigerate until next day.)

Skim (or lift off) and discard fat from soup; bring soup to a simmer. Add okra and parsley; cover and continue to simmer until okra is tender to bite and meat near thighbone is no longer pink when slashed (5 to 10 more minutes).

Ladle gumbo over rice in wide soup bowls. Pass filé to sprinkle over gumbo. Makes 6 to 8 servings.

Chicken Pot-au-Feu

Why steam chicken? It's a method of cooking that leaves meat especially moist...and exceptionally flavorful, too, when you steam vegetables and herbs alongside the chicken, as in this recipe.

Though French in character, this dish cooks in a Chinese Yunnan pot—a lidded clay pot with a cone-shaped spout in the center. (We also give directions for cooking in an ordinary mixing bowl.)

  ¼ cup dry white wine
  2 teaspoons chicken bouillon granules
  2 large leeks (about 1 lb. *total*)
  2 whole chicken legs, thighs attached
    (about 1 lb. *total*), rinsed and patted dry
  4 small thin-skinned potatoes, *each* 1½ to
    2 inches in diameter
  2 large carrots, cut into 3-inch lengths
  2 cloves garlic, crushed
  1 bay leaf
  ½ teaspoon thyme leaves
    Dijon mustard
    Prepared horseradish

In an 8 or 9-inch Yunnan pot or a 2-quart bowl, stir together wine and bouillon granules. Trim and discard ends and tops from leeks, leaving about 3 inches of green leaves. Discard tough outer leaves. Split leeks lengthwise; rinse well, then cut crosswise into 3-inch lengths. Arrange leeks, chicken, potatoes, carrots, garlic, and bay leaf in Yunnan pot or in bowl; sprinkle with thyme.

Place lid on Yunnan pot (if you're using a bowl, leave it uncovered). Place a wire rack in a wok or other deep pan that's wide enough to hold pot or bowl. Carefully set pot or bowl on rack. Pour water into pan until level reaches halfway up sides of pot (if you're using a bowl, pour in water to just beneath rack).

Cover pan and bring water to a boil over high heat. Then reduce heat and steam, adding boiling water as needed to maintain water level, until meat near thighbone is no longer pink when slashed (about 1 hour).

Lift out chicken and vegetables; accompany with mustard and horseradish. Skim and discard fat from broth; serve in cups. Makes 2 servings.

Chicken with Ginger Sauce

If you're looking for a light, fresh entrée, you can't do much better than steamed chicken flavored with sherry, soy, and ginger. (This recipe is also a good choice when you want cooked chicken for salads or sandwiches.)

To highlight the chicken, keep accompaniments simple—you might offer steamed rice to soak up the sauce made from the cooking juices, plus a fresh vegetable.

  2 tablespoons dry sherry or apple juice
  1 tablespoon soy sauce
  1½ teaspoons minced fresh ginger
  1 large clove garlic, minced or pressed
    3 to 3½-pound whole frying chicken
  1 tablespoon *each* cornstarch and water
  ¼ cup thinly sliced green onions
    (including tops)
    Salt and pepper

In a small bowl, combine sherry, soy, ginger, and garlic. Set aside.

Remove chicken neck and giblets; reserve for other uses, if desired. Discard lumps of fat. Rinse chicken inside and out; pat dry. Place chicken, breast down, on a sheet of heavy-duty foil large enough to enclose it. Bring foil up around all sides of chicken, then pour sherry mixture over chicken. Enclose bird in foil, folding it over on top so package can be opened easily to check for doneness.

To cook chicken, use a pan with a steaming insert; or, if you don't have a regular steamer, use a perforated tray or wire rack set on supports (such as tuna cans) inside a deep pan with a tight-fitting lid. Pour enough water into pan to come just under steaming insert (or rack) without touching food. Bring water to a full boil over high heat; then adjust heat to keep water actively boiling.

Place foil-wrapped chicken in steamer, seam side up. Steam until meat near thighbone is no longer pink when slashed (1 to 1¼ hours). Add boiling water as necessary to maintain water level. Transfer chicken to a platter, draining juices back into foil container; keep chicken warm.

Skim and discard fat from juices, then measure; you should have 1¼ cups. (If you have more, boil to reduce; if you have less, add water.) In a 1 to 2-quart pan, stir together cornstarch and the 1 table spoon water; stir in juices. Cook over medium heat, stirring, until sauce boils and thickens. Stir in onions; season to taste with salt and pepper. To serve, spoon some of sauce over chicken; pass remaining sauce at the table to spoon over individual portions of meat. Makes about 4 servings.

Thai Chicken in Coconut Milk

Rich, mellow-sweet coconut milk is often used as a foil for the spicy seasonings of Southeast Asian cuisines. Our version of this tasty poached chicken dish from Thailand uses an authentic-tasting substitute for coconut milk—a combination of half-and-half and coconut extract. In addition to being less costly and more readily available than real coconut milk, this substitute behaves more consistently during cooking.

> 3 to 3½-pound frying chicken, cut up
> 4 cups half-and-half (light cream)
> 2 teaspoons coconut extract
> Spice Paste (recipe follows)
> 2 tablespoons fish sauce or soy sauce
> ¼ teaspoon grated lime peel
> 1 to 3 small dried hot red chiles
> Salt
> Fresh cilantro (coriander) sprigs
> 1 cucumber, scored with a fork and thinly sliced

Reserve chicken neck and giblets for other uses, if desired. Remove and discard skin, if desired; then rinse chicken and pat dry.

Combine half-and-half and coconut extract in a 4 to 5-quart pan. Bring to a boil over high heat, then reduce heat to low. Add chicken, placing breast pieces on top. Regulate heat so liquid barely bubbles; then cover and cook until meat near thighbone is no longer pink when slashed (40 to 45 minutes).

Lift out chicken and drain briefly. Arrange on a heatproof platter, cover, and keep warm in oven at lowest setting. Boil cooking liquid over medium heat, stirring occasionally, until reduced to 1½ cups (about 25 minutes). Meanwhile, prepare Spice Paste.

Stir Spice Paste, fish sauce, lime peel, and chiles into reduced cooking liquid; continue to boil, stirring constantly, for 5 minutes. Remove chiles; season sauce to taste with salt.

To serve, spoon sauce over chicken and garnish with cilantro and cucumber. Makes about 4 servings.

Spice Paste. In a food processor or blender, combine 2 to 4 **small dried hot red chiles;** 1 teaspoon *each* **pepper, ground cumin, ground coriander,** and **ground ginger;** 2 tablespoons grated **lemon peel;** ½ small **onion,** cut into chunks; 1 tablespoon **peanut butter;** and 1 teaspoon **salad oil.** Whirl to a paste, stopping as needed to push ingredients against blade.

Steeped Chicken with Basil Dressing

(Pictured on facing page)

Adapted from a classic Chinese cooking method, steeping involves bringing water to a boil, then turning off the heat and immersing the food in hot water. Unlike traditional poaching, which employs direct heat to keep the water at a simmer, steeping uses only the warmth retained in the hot water.

> 2 whole chicken breasts (about 1 lb. *each*), split
> 2 thin slices *each* lemon and onion
> 1 small slice fresh ginger
> 3 parsley or fresh thyme sprigs
> Ice water
> Basil Dressing (recipe follows)
> Lettuce leaves
> 3 large tomatoes, thinly sliced
> Fresh basil or cilantro (coriander) leaves (optional)

Rinse chicken and pat dry. Place in a 4 to 5-quart pan; pour in enough water to cover chicken by 1 to 2 inches. Lift out chicken; add lemon, onion, ginger, and parsley to water.

Cover pan and bring water to a rolling boil over high heat. Remove from heat and quickly immerse chicken in water. Cover pan tightly and let stand for 18 to 20 minutes; do not uncover until this time is up. To check doneness, slash meat in thickest part; it should no longer look pink. If chicken is not done, return to hot water, cover, and let steep for a few more minutes.

Drain chicken; plunge into ice water to cool quickly. When cold, gently peel off skin and remove meat from bones, keeping chicken pieces whole. Discard skin and bones. (At this point, you may cover and refrigerate for up to 2 days.)

Prepare Basil Dressing. Line ends of a platter with lettuce; arrange tomato slices on top. Slice chicken across the grain about ½ inch thick; arrange in center of platter. Drizzle chicken and tomatoes with a little Basil Dressing. Pass remaining dressing at the table. Garnish with basil leaves, if desired. Makes 4 servings.

Basil Dressing. In a blender or food processor, combine 1 cup lightly packed **fresh basil leaves** (or 3 tablespoons dry basil and ¼ cup chopped parsley), 2 cloves **garlic,** ¼ cup **white wine vinegar,** ½ cup **olive oil** or salad oil, 2 tablespoons grated **Parmesan cheese,** and ⅛ teaspoon **pepper;** whirl until puréed.

There's no cooler choice for a hot summer day than Steeped Chicken with Basil Dressing (facing page). Our refreshing main-dish salad features moist, juicy chicken breasts drizzled with an herb vinaigrette.

Other Glorious Birds

Tempting turkey, duck, game hens & more

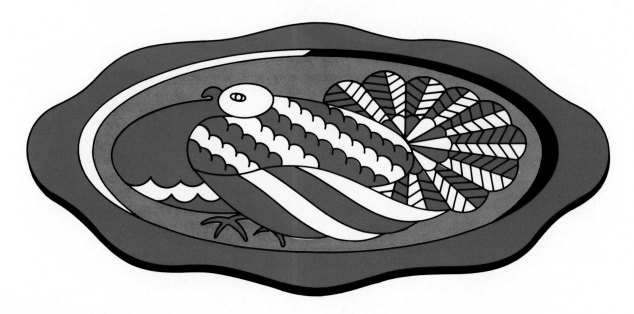

What's your favorite poultry for special occasions? Chances are it's one of the birds in this chapter: turkey for Thanksgiving, goose or duck for Christmas, game hens or even dainty quail or squab for a dinner party. But these "other birds" aren't just for special meals; as their availability increases, they're appearing on menus more often.

Turkey in particular has gained great popularity for everyday meals, since it's now marketed cut up as well as whole. You can buy just a small quantity, choosing only your favorite parts—breast, wings, drumsticks, or thighs. Turkey parts lend themselves to all manner of dishes, from delicate scaloppine to hearty dark-meat casseroles; and like chicken, they're very reasonably priced. Of course, whole turkey is still the top choice for holidays and celebrations—and we include recipes for basic roast turkey (in the oven and on the barbecue), savory stuffings, and the best gravy ever.

Available both fresh and frozen, game hens are sold as widely as chicken. Served half to a diner, they're an attractive light entrée; for heartier appetites, add a stuffing or allow a whole bird for each person.

Extra rich flavor makes duck and goose favorites with many diners. Like whole turkeys, these all-dark-meat birds are often sold frozen. Goose may be a bit harder to locate than duck; in many parts of the country, it's seasonal and must be specially ordered (check service meat markets in your area for details).

Special ordering may also be necessary to obtain quail, chukar, pheasant, and squab, though these birds are becoming easier to find. They're still relatively expensive, but worth it when you want an impressive presentation.

Roast Turkey

(Pictured on page 62)

For many people, the holidays wouldn't seem complete without at least one roast turkey dinner. Favorite accompaniments vary, but top billing always goes to the plump golden bird—usually served with savory stuffing and gravy made from the pan drippings.

Our basic oven-roasted turkey is perfect for a traditional holiday meal. For something just a bit different, you might try Roast Turkey & Vegetables. And if you enjoy barbecued poultry, our barbecued whole turkey is well worth a try. The meat has a wonderful smoky flavor—and while the turkey roasts on the barbecue, your oven is free for cooking other foods.

The size of bird you choose depends on the number of diners to be served (and on your fondness for leftovers). As a rule of thumb, figure on ¾ to 1 pound of turkey (bone-in) per person.

For best results with any size of turkey, keep the following points in mind (see also the tips on page 13). If the turkey is frozen, thaw it completely before cooking as directed on page 93. Never stuff a turkey until just before roasting; remove the stuffing soon after the bird is done. Finally, even if the turkey comes equipped with a pop-up thermometer, check doneness with a meat thermometer (it's more accurate).

> **Stuffing of your choice** (optional; see pages 64 and 65 for recipes and amounts)
> **8 to 30-pound turkey** (thawed if frozen)
> **Butter or margarine,** softened
> **Foolproof Turkey Gravy** (optional; page 72)

Prepare stuffing, if desired; set aside.

Remove turkey neck and giblets; reserve for Foolproof Turkey Gravy or other uses, if desired. Rinse turkey inside and out and pat dry, then stuff and truss (see page 65). Rub turkey all over with butter.

Place turkey, breast down, on a rack in a large, shallow roasting pan. Roast, uncovered, in a 325° oven, turning breast up halfway through cooking, until a meat thermometer inserted in thickest part of thigh (not touching bone) registers 185°F or until meat near thighbone is no longer pink when slashed. (Roasting times vary depending on size of turkey; consult the chart on page 13.) While turkey roasts, begin preparing Foolproof Turkey Gravy, if desired.

If turkey is stuffed, spoon stuffing into a serving bowl and keep warm. Transfer turkey to a plat-

ter; keep warm. Finish preparing gravy. To serve, carve turkey as directed on page 94; pass stuffing and gravy at the table. Makes 8 to 30 servings.

Roast Turkey & Vegetables

Prepare stuffed or unstuffed 12 to 14-pound turkey as directed for **Roast Turkey,** but place turkey, breast down, directly in a large (at least 11½ by 17 inches), shallow roasting pan (not on a rack). Place pan on lowest rack of oven.

About 1½ hours before turkey is done, turn it breast up. Then place 4 or 5 medium-size unpeeled **onions** in roasting pan around turkey; also place 8 to 10 slender **sweet potatoes** or yams (pierced in several places with a fork) on oven rack above turkey.

About 1 hour before turkey is done, drain 2 cans (15½ oz. *each*) **whole chestnuts in water;** scatter in pan around turkey, pushing down into pan juices. Seed 4 or 5 large **red or green bell peppers;** tuck into pan around turkey. At end of roasting time, onions and sweet potatoes should give readily when gently squeezed; bell peppers should be tender when pierced, but not limp.

To serve, carve turkey as directed on page 94. Cut each onion and bell pepper in half lengthwise. Slit tops of sweet potatoes; add a pat of **butter** or margarine to each. Lift chestnuts from pan with a slotted spoon; place in a serving dish. Makes 8 to 10 servings (you'll have leftover turkey).

Whole Roast Turkey on the Barbecue

About 45 minutes before cooking, start barbecue fire (see "Barbecuing with Indirect Heat," page 37). Meanwhile, prepare stuffed or unstuffed turkey as directed for **Roast Turkey;** also prepare **Turkey Baste** (recipe follows). Place turkey, breast down, in middle of grill over drip pan. Cover barbecue and adjust dampers.

Cook, turning turkey breast up halfway through cooking, until a meat thermometer inserted in thickest portion of thigh (not touching bone) registers 185°F or until meat near thighbone is no longer pink when slashed. During last 1½ hours of cooking, brush bird frequently with **Turkey Baste.** (Consult the chart of roasting times and temperatures on page 13 for approximate cooking time; barbecued turkeys cook in about the same time as do oven-roasted birds.)

Turkey Baste. Melt ¼ cup **butter** or margarine in a small pan over medium heat. Remove from heat and stir in ½ cup **dry sherry** or apple juice and ½ teaspoon *each* **dry rosemary, paprika,** and **rubbed sage.**

Center stage at a holiday feast, Roast Turkey (page 61) brings rounds
of applause. Choose your favorite stuffing (see pages 64 and 65) to
bake inside the bird and beneath the golden brown skin at the neck.

Barbecued Butterflied Turkey with Under-the-skin Stuffing

A layer of stuffing tucked beneath the skin helps keep this bird's breast meat extra moist.

**Leek-Lemon Stuffing (page 64) or about
5 cups other stuffing
10 to 12-pound turkey (thawed if frozen)**

Prepare stuffing and set aside. About 45 minutes before cooking, start barbecue fire (see "Barbecuing with Indirect Heat," page 37).

Meanwhile, remove turkey neck and giblets; reserve for other uses, if desired. With poultry shears or a knife, split turkey lengthwise along one side of backbone. Pull turkey open; place, skin side up, on a flat surface and press firmly, cracking breastbone slightly, until bird lies reasonably flat. Rinse and pat dry.

Next, separate skin from meat over entire breast. Starting at neck end, ease your hands gently under skin to loosen it; complete separation process from other end of breast, working carefully to avoid tearing skin. Using your hands, insert an even layer of dressing between meat and skin. Tuck excess neck skin under breastbone.

Place turkey, skin side up, in middle of grill over drip pan. Loosely cover breast with foil to prevent overbrowning. Cover barbecue and adjust dampers. Cook turkey until a meat thermometer inserted in thickest portion of thigh (not touching bone) registers 185°F or until meat near thighbone is no longer pink when slashed (1½ to 2 hours). Remove foil 30 minutes before turkey is done.

Transfer turkey to a platter. To carve breast, first cut off wings; then cut under breast along rib bones to free meat. Starting near wing joint, cut through dressing and breast meat to make ¾-inch-thick slices. Makes 10 to 12 servings.

Turkey-Pineapple Skewers

Chunks of turkey breast skewered with fresh pineapple make a tropical-tasting entrée.

**2½ pounds boned turkey breast, skinned
¼ cup butter or margarine
⅓ cup dry sherry
½ teaspoon *each* paprika, sage leaves, dry rosemary, and thyme leaves
1 small pineapple (3 to 3½ lbs.)**

Rinse turkey, pat dry, and cut into 1½-inch chunks. Melt butter in a small pan; stir in sherry, paprika, sage, rosemary, and thyme. Pour butter mixture into a large bowl; add turkey and stir to coat. Cover and let stand for 1 hour.

Peel and core pineapple, then cut into 1½-inch chunks. Lift turkey from marinade and drain briefly (reserve marinade). Thread turkey and pineapple chunks alternately on about 7 bamboo or metal skewers (each about 12 inches long), beginning and ending with turkey.

Arrange skewers on a rack in a large broiler pan. Broil 6 inches below heat, basting with marinade every few minutes and turning halfway through cooking, until turkey is no longer pink when slashed (about 15 minutes *total*). Makes about 6 servings.

Grilled Turkey Steaks with Cashew Butter

Marinate the turkey in advance; at serving time, you need only make the sauce and grill the meat.

**2½ pounds boned turkey breast, skinned
⅔ cup dry sherry
2 teaspoons chicken bouillon granules
¼ teaspoon dry rosemary
Cashew Butter (recipe follows)
¼ cup butter or margarine, melted
Parsley sprigs and lemon wedges**

Rinse turkey and pat dry. Cut across the grain into ⅜-inch-thick slices. In a large, shallow baking dish, combine sherry, bouillon granules, and rosemary. Stir to dissolve bouillon. Add turkey and turn to coat. Cover and refrigerate until next day.

About 40 minutes before cooking, start barbecue fire (see "Barbecuing with Direct Heat," page 39). Prepare Cashew Butter and set aside.

Lift turkey from marinade and drain briefly (discard marinade). Place turkey on grill 4 to 6 inches above a solid bed of medium-glowing coals. Cook, turning and basting occasionally with plain melted butter, until meat is no longer pink when slashed (about 8 minutes). Transfer to a platter. Pour Cashew Butter over turkey, then garnish with parsley and lemon wedges. Makes 6 to 8 servings.

Cashew Butter. In a small pan, melt ⅓ cup **butter** or margarine. Add 2 teaspoons **lemon juice** and ½ cup coarsely chopped **salted cashews**. Set at side of grill to keep warm.

Stuffing Recipes & Techniques

Our old-fashioned bread stuffings and lighter vegetable stuffings are as delicious in chicken and game hens as they are in turkey. We don't recommend stuffing goose, duck, or small birds such as quail and squab, though. The natural fat from goose and duck can leave stuffing greasy, and quail and squab cook so briefly that stuffing won't be cooked by the time the meat is done.

For chicken, game hens, or turkey (up to 14 lbs.), allow about ¾ cup stuffing for each pound of poultry. For turkeys over 14 pounds, allow ½ cup stuffing per pound. Use any of these recipes, or choose from other stuffings listed in the index.

You can prepare stuffing up to a day in advance, then cover and refrigerate it. But to avoid any danger of food poisoning, *do not* stuff the bird until just before cooking. Spoon out all the stuffing after the bird is cooked; cover and refrigerate any leftovers.

As the bird cooks, the stuffing will expand, so pack it into the cavities lightly. Place any stuffing you can't fit into the bird in a lightly greased baking dish (or in a double thickness of foil, if you're barbecuing); sprinkle with a little broth, then cover. Cook alongside the bird during the last 45 minutes of cooking.

Old-fashioned Bread Stuffing

Use day-old bread for this stuffing; if made with soft, fresh bread, it turns mushy with cooking.

- ¾ cup (¼ lb. plus ¼ cup) butter or margarine
- 3 large onions, chopped
- 1½ teaspoons marjoram leaves
- ¾ teaspoon *each* pepper, ground sage, and thyme leaves
- 12 cups day-old whole wheat or white bread (or some of each), in ½-inch cubes
- 2 cups chopped celery (including leaves)
- ½ cup chopped parsley
-   Salt

Melt ½ cup of the butter in a wide frying pan over medium heat. Add onions and cook, stirring occasionally, until soft and golden (about 15 minutes). Add remaining ¼ cup butter, marjoram, pepper, sage, and thyme. Remove from heat; stir until butter is melted.

In a 5-quart container, combine bread, celery, and parsley; add onion mixture. With your hands or 2 spoons, toss until well combined. Season to taste with salt. Let cool. Makes about 14 cups.

Oyster Stuffing

Follow directions for **Old-fashioned Bread Stuffing,** but use only 10 cups bread cubes. Add 2 jars (8 to 10 oz. *each*) **oysters,** drained and chopped, to bread cube mixture.

Chestnut Stuffing

Follow directions for **Old-fashioned Bread Stuffing,** but use only 11 cups bread cubes. Add 1 can (15½ oz.) **whole chestnuts in water,** drained and chopped, to bread cube mixture.

Leek-Lemon Stuffing

This all-vegetable dressing is a simple mixture of pine nuts, leeks, and onions, flavored with lemon and tarragon. It's a good choice for Barbecued Butterflied Turkey with Under-the-skin Stuffing (page 63) because it doesn't crumble apart when the meat and stuffing are sliced together.

- ¼ cup butter or margarine
- ⅓ cup pine nuts or slivered almonds
- 2 large onions, thinly sliced
- 7 large leeks (about 3½ lbs. *total*)
- 2 cloves garlic, minced or pressed
- 1½ teaspoons dry tarragon
- 1½ teaspoons grated lemon peel
- 2 tablespoons lemon juice
-   Salt

Melt butter in a 12 to 14-inch frying pan over low heat. Add pine nuts and cook, stirring, until golden (about 1 minute). Lift out nuts with a slotted spoon and set aside on paper towels to drain.

Increase heat to medium. Add onions to pan; cook, stirring occasionally, until soft. Meanwhile, trim and discard ends and tops from leeks, leaving about 3 inches of green leaves. Discard tough outer leaves. Split leeks lengthwise; rinse well, then thinly slice cross-wise (you should have 9 cups).

Add leeks, garlic, and tarragon to pan. Continue to cook, stirring occasionally, until leeks are very soft (about 15 more minutes). Add lemon peel, lemon juice, and pine nuts; season to taste with salt. Let cool. Makes about 5 cups.

Cabbage & Bell Pepper Stuffing

Slightly spicy Italian sausage accents a savory blend of sautéed bell peppers, cabbage, celery, and onions. For a nippier stuffing, substitute hot Italian sausage for mild sausage.

  1½ **pounds mild Italian sausage, casings removed**
   2 **large onions, chopped**
   6 **stalks celery, thinly sliced**
   2 **large red or green bell peppers, seeded and diced**
   4 **quarts coarsely shredded green cabbage (about 3 lbs.)**
   3 **tablespoons butter or margarine**
  ¾ **teaspoon *each* thyme, oregano, and sage leaves**
   3 **eggs, beaten**
  ½ **cup fine dry bread crumbs**
      Salt and pepper

Crumble sausage into a 12 to 14-inch frying pan. Add onions and cook over medium-high heat, stirring, until sausage is browned. Add celery, bell peppers, and half the cabbage. Cook, stirring, until cabbage is wilted; pour into a large bowl.

Melt butter in pan. Add remaining cabbage and cook, stirring, until wilted. Add to sausage-vegetable mixture along with thyme, oregano, sage, eggs, and bread crumbs; blend well. Season to taste with salt and pepper. Let cool. Makes about 12 cups.

Stuffing Techniques

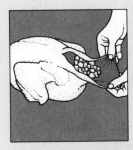
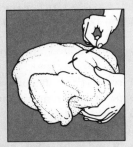

Left: Place bird breast down; lightly fill neck cavity with stuffing. **Right:** Fasten neck skin to back with a metal skewer, closing cavity securely.

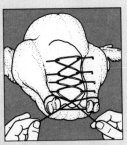

Left: Turn bird over. (If turkey has a wire clamp, squeeze it to remove.) Loosely pack body cavity with stuffing. **Right:** Tuck in tail, then fold skin over cavity; close with metal skewers. Using white cotton string, lace up like a boot and tie. If desired, wrap and tie string around ends of drumsticks for a more compact appearance.

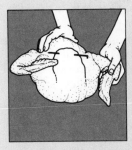
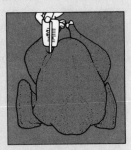

Left: Place bird, breast down, on a rack in a roasting pan; bend wings akimbo. **Right:** Halfway through cooking, turn bird over; insert a meat thermometer in thickest part of thigh (not touching bone).

Turkey Scaloppine with Prosciutto, Gruyère & Peas

(Pictured on facing page)

Delicate-flavored turkey breast makes an economical alternative to veal for scaloppine.

> 1 pound boned turkey breast, skinned
> All-purpose flour
> ½ cup (¼ lb.) butter or margarine
> ½ pound medium-size mushrooms
> ½ cup Marsala
> Salt and pepper
> ¼ pound thinly sliced prosciutto
> 1 cup (4 oz.) shredded Gruyère or Swiss cheese
> Hot cooked peas

Rinse turkey, pat dry, and cut across the grain into ¼-inch-thick slices. Place slices one at a time between 2 sheets of plastic wrap and pound with a flat-surfaced mallet until about ⅛ inch thick. Dip pieces in flour to coat; shake off excess.

Melt 2 tablespoons of the butter in a wide frying pan over medium-high heat. Add turkey, a portion at a time, without crowding; cook, turning once, until meat is lightly browned on both sides (about 1 minute *total*). Add more butter, a tablespoon at a time, as needed to prevent sticking. As turkey is cooked, arrange on an ovenproof platter, slightly overlapping slices; keep warm.

Add mushrooms to pan and cook, stirring, until lightly browned. Pour in Marsala and stir to scrape browned bits free. With a slotted spoon, lift mushrooms from pan; arrange next to turkey.

Boil pan juices over high heat, stirring, until large, shiny bubbles form. Add remaining butter and stir constantly until completely blended. Remove pan from heat; season sauce to taste with salt and pepper. Keep warm.

Top turkey evenly with prosciutto and cheese. Broil about 6 inches below heat just until cheese is melted (2 to 3 minutes). Pour sauce around edge of platter, allowing it to run beneath turkey; spoon peas around turkey. Makes 4 servings.

Turkey Scaloppine with Lemon Caper Sauce

Prepare and cook turkey as directed for **Turkey Scaloppine with Prosciutto, Gruyère & Peas.** Omit mushrooms, Marsala, prosciutto, Gruyère, and peas; instead, after cooking turkey, add 2 tablespoons **lemon juice,** ½ cup **water,** and 1 teaspoon **capers** to pan. Stir to scrape browned bits free.

Bring sauce to a rolling boil. Add remaining butter and finish preparing sauce as directed. Immediately pour sauce over turkey; garnish with **parsley sprigs** and paper-thin **lemon slices.**

Turkey & White Bean Casserole

If you're using turkey thighs for this hearty oven dinner, cut each in half before cooking by slicing it lengthwise right alongside the bone.

> 1 package (16 oz.) dried Great Northern beans
> 14 cups water
> 6 slices bacon, diced
> 4 pounds turkey thighs or drumsticks
> ½ cup dry white wine
> 2 large onions, chopped
> 3 cloves garlic, minced or pressed
> 4 medium-size carrots, cut into ¼-inch-thick slices
> 2 stalks celery, sliced
> 1 can (14½ oz.) pear-shaped tomatoes
> 1½ teaspoons dry rosemary
> Salt and pepper

Sort beans and remove any debris; rinse well and drain. In a large pan, bring 8 cups of the water to a boil over high heat; add beans and boil, uncovered, for 2 minutes. Remove from heat, cover, and let stand for 1 hour. Drain beans, then return to pan and add remaining 6 cups water. Bring to a boil over high heat; reduce heat, cover, and simmer until beans are tender to bite (about 1½ hours). Drain and set aside.

In a wide frying pan, cook bacon over medium heat until crisp. Lift out, drain, and set aside; leave drippings in pan. Increase heat to medium-high. Add turkey to pan, a portion at a time, without crowding; cook, turning, until browned on all sides. Transfer to a 6-quart casserole or ovenproof pan; pour in wine. Cover and bake in a 350° oven for 1 hour.

Meanwhile, add onions and garlic to drippings in frying pan; cook over medium-high heat, stirring, until onions are soft. Add carrots, celery, tomatoes (break up with a spoon) and their liquid, rosemary, and beans. Bring to a boil, then season to taste with salt and pepper.

After turkey has baked for 1 hour, stir hot bean mixture into casserole; cover and continue to bake until meat near bone is no longer pink when slashed (45 to 60 more minutes). Let stand for about 15 minutes, then sprinkle with bacon and serve. Makes about 8 servings.

Peeking out from beneath a crown of melted cheese, sliced boneless turkey breast makes an elegant entrée: Italian-style Turkey
Scaloppine with Prosciutto, Gruyère & Peas (facing page).

67

Specialty Birds

A tasty choice for a festive occasion is the farm-raised specialty bird. Here, we feature four kinds: quail, squab (young pigeon), pheasant, and chukar (a type of partridge). These birds are much more tender than their wild counterparts—and none has a gamy flavor. Chukar and pheasant are all-white-meat birds that taste rather like chicken; quail and squab—all dark meat—have a more intense flavor.

Fresh and frozen quail and squab are becoming more common in supermarkets. Finding the other birds may take a little sleuthing; try service meat markets or go directly to game farms if there are any in your area (check listings under "Poultry" and "Game" in the Yellow Pages). Many game farms sell birds by mail order; look in cooking magazines for advertisements.

To get full benefit of these birds' fine flavor, and to ensure that meat is moist and succulent, cook the birds briefly at high temperatures. *To check for doneness, slash meat in thickest portion of breast—it should look moist but not wet. Quail and squab will still be red; chukar and pheasant will be white with a touch of pink at the bone.*

Quail Pie

Bringing to mind the nursery rhyme, these birds are baked with vegetables in a double-crust pie. When you serve the dish, suggest the option of eating it by hand, and supply plenty of napkins.

  8 **quail (3 to 4 oz.** *each*)**, thawed if frozen**
  1 **pound spinach, stems removed**
  4 **tablespoons butter or margarine**
  1 **large onion, chopped**
  2 **large carrots, chopped**
  ½ **pound small mushrooms, quartered**
  1 **tablespoon all-purpose flour**
     Pastry for a double-crust 10-inch pie
  1 **egg beaten with 1 tablespoon water**
  1 **cup whipping cream**
  ½ **cup dry sherry**

Remove quail necks and giblets; reserve for other uses, if desired. Rinse quail inside and out, pat dry, and set aside.

Rinse spinach well; place with water that clings to leaves in a 12 to 14-inch frying pan. Cover and cook over medium-high heat, stirring once, until spinach is wilted. Pour into a colander and let cool; squeeze out excess moisture.

Wipe frying pan clean; add 2 tablespoons of the butter and melt over medium-high heat. Add quail, a portion at a time, without crowding; cook, turning, until browned on all sides. Remove from pan and set aside.

Melt remaining 2 tablespoons butter in pan; add onion and carrots and cook, stirring, until onion is soft. Add mushrooms and cook, stirring, for 1 minute. Add flour and cook, stirring, until bubbly; set aside.

On a floured board, roll out half the pastry to a 14-inch circle. Fit pastry circle into a 10-inch pie pan; trim edges to 1 inch beyond rim. Spoon mushroom mixture into pastry; top evenly with spinach. Arrange quail spoke-fashion on spinach, breasts up and legs toward edges of pan.

Roll out remaining pastry to a circle at least 13 inches in diameter. Drape pastry over quail, allowing legs to poke through. Trim edges of top crust, then crimp edges of pastry to seal. Brush top with egg-water mixture. Bake pie, uncovered, on lowest rack of a 400° oven until richly browned (about 30 minutes).

In a wide frying pan, bring cream and sherry to a boil over high heat. Boil, stirring, until reduced to ¾ cup. To serve, cut pie between birds into 8 wedges. Spoon sherry sauce over individual portions. Makes 8 servings.

Pheasant Jeweled with Fruit

Green grapes, pomegranate seeds, and tiny onions glisten like jewels, making a perfect setting for roast pheasant. Because the bird roasts only briefly, you begin by sautéing it in butter to give the skin a pleasing golden color.

2½-pound pheasant (thawed if frozen)
4 tablespoons butter or margarine
10 to 15 small white boiling onions (*each* about 1½ inches in diameter)
½ cup water
1½ to 2 cups seedless green grapes
½ to 1 cup pomegranate seeds (optional)
½ teaspoon cornstarch
⅓ cup sour cream
½ cup regular-strength beef broth
2 tablespoons brandy
⅛ teaspoon dry tarragon

Remove pheasant neck and giblets; reserve for other uses, if desired. Rinse bird inside and out and pat dry.

Melt 2 tablespoons of the butter in a wide frying pan over medium-high heat. Add pheasant; cook, turning, until browned on all sides.

Place pheasant, breast up, on a rack in a shallow roasting pan. Roast in a 450° oven until bird tests done (about 25 minutes; see instructions on facing page).

Meanwhile, melt remaining 2 tablespoons butter in frying pan over medium heat. Add onions and cook, turning frequently, until golden. Add water; cover and cook until onions are just tender when pierced and liquid has evaporated (about 20 minutes). Add grapes and pomegranate seeds (if desired); stir until warmed.

Drain juices from pheasant into roasting pan, then transfer pheasant to a platter. Arrange onions and fruit alongside and keep warm. Stir together cornstarch and sour cream; add to roasting pan with broth, brandy, and tarragon. Boil over high heat, stirring constantly, until sauce is reduced to ½ cup. Pour into a serving bowl; pass at the table to spoon over individual portions of meat, onions, and fruit. Makes 2 or 3 servings.

Squab, Chukar, or Quail with Pears & Red Wine Sauce

Pears poached in red wine beautifully complement the flavor of roasted poultry in this special-occasion recipe. You can take your choice of three specialty birds (or just use the kind most readily available to you). For an especially grand presentation, spoon hot wild rice evenly over a platter; arrange the birds around the rim and place the pears in the center. Pass the buttery wine sauce to spoon over each serving.

1½ cups dry red wine
¼ cup sugar
¾ teaspoon whole black peppercorns
3 medium-size firm-ripe Bosc or Comice pears
6 squab or chukar (12 to 16 oz. *each*), thawed if frozen; or 12 to 18 quail, (3 to 4 oz. *each*), thawed if frozen
⅔ cup butter or margarine
⅓ cup minced shallots or mild red onion
¾ cup regular-strength beef broth

In a 4 to 5-quart pan, combine wine, sugar, and peppercorns. Peel pears, cut in half lengthwise, and core; add to wine mixture. Bring to a boil over high heat; then reduce heat, cover, and simmer, turning fruit several times, until pears are tender when pierced (about 7 minutes). Set aside.

Remove necks and giblets from birds; reserve for other uses, if desired. Rinse birds inside and out and pat dry. Melt 2 tablespoons of the butter in a wide frying pan over medium-high heat. Add birds, a portion at a time, without crowding. Cook, turning, until browned on all sides; if necessary, add 1 more tablespoon butter to prevent sticking.

Place birds, breast up, on a rack in a large, shallow roasting pan. Roast in a 400° oven until meat tests done (12 to 15 minutes for quail, 20 to 25 minutes for squab or chukar; see instructions on facing page).

Drain juices from birds into roasting pan. Transfer birds to a large platter; lift pears from poaching liquid and arrange alongside birds. Keep warm.

Pour roasting pan drippings into frying pan, add shallots, and stir over high heat for 1 minute. Add broth and ¾ cup of the pear poaching liquid (discard any remaining poaching liquid). Boil rapidly until sauce is reduced to ⅔ cup. Reduce heat to low and add remaining butter all at once; stir constantly until butter melts and blends into sauce. Strain sauce into a small bowl; pass at the table to spoon over individual portions. Makes 6 servings.

Barbecued to sizzling perfection, plump Apricot-glazed Game Hens (facing page) are practically a meal in themselves. Serve the butterflied birds one to a diner, with small thin-skinned potatoes.

Crusty Oven-fried Turkey Parts

Parmesan cheese and seasoned croutons make a crisp coating for turkey. Depending on what's available, you can use turkey drumsticks, thighs, or wings (or try a combination of the three).

    4 pounds turkey parts—drumsticks,
       thighs, or wings (each piece
       about 1 lb.)
    ⅓ cup all-purpose flour
    ½ teaspoon paprika
    ¼ teaspoon pepper
    2 eggs
    2 tablespoons milk
    2 cups seasoned croutons, crushed
    ⅓ cup grated Parmesan cheese
    ¼ cup butter or margarine, melted

Rinse turkey; pat dry. In a bag, combine flour, paprika, and pepper. Beat eggs and milk in a 9-inch pie pan; mix croutons and cheese on a rimmed plate.

Shake turkey pieces, one at a time, in seasoned flour; then dip in egg mixture, spooning it over turkey to coat well, if necessary. Drain briefly and roll in crouton mixture to coat evenly. Place on an ungreased 10 by 15-inch rimmed baking pan. Sprinkle any remaining crouton mixture over turkey pieces. Cover tightly with foil.

Bake in a 350° oven for 1¼ hours. Remove foil and drizzle turkey with butter. Continue to bake, uncovered, until meat near bone is no longer pink when slashed and coating is crisp (20 to 30 more minutes). Makes about 4 servings.

Apricot-glazed Game Hens

(Pictured on facing page)

Apricot jam, orange-flavored liqueur, and a savory herb butter season these birds.

       Herb Butter (recipe follows)
    4 Rock Cornish game hens (1¼ to 1½ lbs.
       each), thawed if frozen
    ¼ cup apricot jam
    1 tablespoon orange-flavored liqueur
       Watercress sprigs

About 40 minutes before cooking, start barbecue fire (see "Barbecuing with Direct Heat," page 39).

Prepare Herb Butter; set aside. Remove game hen necks and giblets; reserve for other uses, if

desired. With poultry shears or a knife, split hens lengthwise along one side of backbone. Pull hens open; place, skin side up, on a flat surface and press firmly, cracking bones slightly, until hens lie reasonably flat. Rinse and pat dry.

Brush hens all over with Herb Butter; then place, skin side up, on grill 4 to 6 inches above a solid bed of medium-glowing coals. Cook for 15 minutes, turning and brushing occasionally with any remaining Herb Butter.

Meanwhile, stir jam in a small pan over medium-low heat until melted; stir in liqueur. Brush evenly over hens and continue to cook, turning occasionally, until meat near thighbone is no longer pink when slashed (about 15 more minutes). Garnish with watercress. Makes 4 to 8 servings.

Herb Butter. In a pan, melt ⅓ cup **butter** or margarine with ¼ teaspoon *each* **dry rosemary** and **dry tarragon** and ⅛ teaspoon **white pepper.** Remove from heat and stir in 1 tablespoon **lemon juice.**

Grilled Game Hens with Jalapeño Jelly Glaze

Lime juice and peppery jalapeño jelly glaze these game hens. (You'll find the jelly in specialty food stores and some delicatessens.)

    6 Rock Cornish game hens (1¼ to 1½
       lbs. *each*), thawed if frozen
       Pepper
    1 jar (about 7½ oz.) jalapeño jelly
    ¼ cup butter or margarine
    2 tablespoons lime juice

About 40 minutes before cooking, start barbecue fire (see "Barbecuing with Direct Heat," page 39). Remove game hen necks and giblets; reserve for other uses, if desired. With poultry shears or a knife, split hens lengthwise along one side of backbone. Pull hens open; place, skin side up, on a flat surface and press firmly, cracking bones slightly, until hens lie reasonably flat. Rinse and pat dry. Sprinkle with pepper.

In a 1 to 2-quart pan, stir jelly and butter over medium-high heat until melted. Stir in lime juice; set aside. Place hens, skin side up, on grill 4 to 6 inches above a solid bed of medium-glowing coals. Cook, turning occasionally, for 20 minutes; then baste with jelly mixture. Continue to cook, basting and turning occasionally, until meat near thighbone is no longer pink when slashed (about 10 more minutes). Makes 6 to 12 servings.

Foolproof Turkey Gravy

Rich brown gravy is the perfect accompaniment for roast turkey. This recipe makes 4 cups; if you want more, just double it.

        Turkey neck and giblets
    4 cups regular-strength chicken broth,
        homemade (page 53) or purchased
    1 small onion, sliced
    1 large carrot, cut into chunks
    1 stalk celery, cut into chunks
    1 parsley sprig
        Turkey drippings from roasting
        pan or barbecue drip pan
        Melted butter or margarine
    ½ cup all-purpose flour
        Salt and pepper

Place turkey neck and giblets (except liver) in a 2-quart pan; add broth, onion, carrot, celery, and parsley. Bring to a boil over high heat; reduce heat, cover, and simmer until gizzard is tender when pierced (1½ hours). Add liver; cook for 5 more minutes.

Lift out neck and giblets; set aside. Strain broth (discard vegetables), then measure; you should have about 4 cups.

Add 1 cup of the broth to pan drippings; stir over medium heat to scrape browned bits free. Pour into a large glass measure; set aside to let fat rise to the top. Meanwhile, finely chop neck meat and giblets; set aside.

Skim fat from dripping mixture and discard all but ½ cup of fat. (If you have less than ½ cup, add melted butter to bring up to this amount.) Set aside. Add enough of remaining broth to dripping mixture to make 4 cups liquid.

Combine the ½ cup turkey fat and flour in a 2-quart pan. Cook over medium heat, stirring, until bubbly. Remove from heat. Gradually pour in broth-dripping mixture, stirring constantly with a wire whisk until smooth. Return pan to medium heat and cook, stirring, until gravy boils and thickens. Stir in neck meat and giblets; season to taste with salt and pepper. Makes about 4 cups.

Herb-Cheese Game Hens

Baked inside game hens, creamy cheese flavored with garlic and herbs makes a tasty dip to scoop up with chunks of crusty bread.

    2 Rock Cornish game hens (1½ lbs. *each*),
        thawed if frozen
        Pepper and ground nutmeg
    1 package (4 to 5 oz.) creamy appetizer
        cheese flavored with garlic and herbs
    2 tablespoons butter or margarine, melted
        Cherry tomatoes
        Crusty French bread

Remove game hen necks and giblets; reserve for other uses, if desired. Rinse hens inside and out; pat dry. Lightly sprinkle with pepper and nutmeg. Cut cheese into 2 equal portions; place one portion in body cavity of each hen. Truss body cavities, then bend wings akimbo (see page 65).

Place hens, breast down, on a rack in a shallow roasting pan. Brush with butter. Roast, uncovered, in a 425° oven for 30 minutes. Turn hens over, baste with pan drippings, and continue to roast until meat near thighbone is no longer pink when slashed (20 to 30 more minutes).

To serve, place birds on plates and snip each in half with poultry shears. Garnish with tomatoes; offer bread to scoop up cheese. Makes 2 servings.

Spinach-stuffed Game Hens

Use extra stuffing as a side dish or as a decorative bed for these elegant little birds.

        Spinach-Rice Stuffing (page 36)
        Green Onion Butter (page 43)
    2 Rock Cornish game hens (1½ lbs. *each*),
        thawed if frozen

Prepare stuffing and Green Onion Butter; set aside. Remove game hen necks and giblets; reserve for other uses, if desired. Rinse hens inside and out; pat dry, then stuff, truss, and bend wings akimbo (see page 65). Spoon remaining stuffing into a greased 5 by 9-inch loaf pan. Cover with foil and heat in oven during last 25 minutes of roasting.

Place hens, breast down, on a rack in a shallow roasting pan. Brush with Green Onion Butter. Roast, uncovered, in a 425° oven for 30 minutes. Brush hens with Green Onion Butter, then turn over and continue to roast, basting occasionally with Green Onion Butter, until meat near thighbone is no longer pink when slashed (20 to 30 more minutes).

To serve, snip each bird in half with poultry shears. Makes 4 servings.

Barbecued Duck with Hoisin

Skinned duck pieces, spicy with hoisin, cook on the grill; the skin bakes crisp in the oven.

> 2 **ducklings (4 to 5 lbs. *each*), thawed if frozen**
> 1 **cup hoisin sauce**
> ½ **cup raspberry or red wine vinegar**
> ½ **cup orange juice**
>   **Baked Duck Skin (optional; recipe follows)**

Remove duckling necks and giblets; reserve for other uses, if desired. Discard lumps of fat. Rinse ducklings inside and out and pat dry. With a sharp knife, cut legs from body at hip joints (near center back); also cut wings from breast. Pull skin off breast and trim breast meat from ribs, sliding knife parallel to bones. Reserve carcass for other uses, or discard. If desired, cover and refrigerate skin to use for Baked Duck Skin.

In a large bowl, stir together hoisin, vinegar, and orange juice. Add duck pieces and turn to coat. Cover and refrigerate for at least 6 hours or until next day, turning several times.

About 45 minutes before cooking, start barbecue fire (see "Barbecuing with Indirect Heat," page 37). Begin baking duck skin, if desired.

Lift duck pieces from marinade and drain briefly (reserve marinade). Set breast pieces aside. Place legs and wings in middle of grill over drip pan. Cover barbecue, adjust dampers, and cook for 30 minutes, basting once with marinade after 15 minutes.

Uncover barbecue. Place breast pieces directly over coals (not over drip pan) and cook, turning after 5 minutes, until meat in thickest portion is no longer red when slashed (it should still look pink) —about 10 minutes *total*. Meat near thighbone should be firm but still slightly pink. Serve duck pieces with Baked Duck Skin, if desired. Makes 4 to 6 servings.

Baked Duck Skin. Cut **duck skin** into pieces about 4 inches square. Arrange in a single layer, fat side down, on a wire rack in a rimmed baking pan. Bake in a 350° oven until crisp (about 45 minutes).

Tangerine-sauced Roast Duck

For this recipe, you need to leave enough room around the roasting rack to fit yam chunks and onions in the pan. Use a V-shaped rack, or set a regular-size flat rack in a large pan.

> 4 to 5-pound duckling (thawed if frozen)
> 1 **bay leaf**
> 1½ **cups water**
> 1 **small onion, quartered**
> 2 or 3 **medium-size onions (unpeeled)**
> 1½ **pounds yams, peeled and cut into 2-inch pieces**
> 1½ **teaspoons slivered tangerine peel**
> ¾ **cup tangerine juice (about 2 large tangerines)**
> 1½ **tablespoons honey**
> 2 **teaspoons *each* cornstarch and water**
>   **Salt and pepper**
>   **Thin strips of tangerine peel (optional)**

Remove duckling neck and giblets. Reserve liver for other uses, if desired; set aside neck and remaining giblets for use in sauce. Discard lumps of fat. Rinse duckling inside and out and pat dry. With a fork, prick skin all over at 1-inch intervals. Place duckling, breast down, on a V-shaped rack in a shallow roasting pan. Roast, uncovered, in a 375° oven for 1 hour.

Meanwhile, in a 1 to 1½-quart pan, combine neck, giblets, bay leaf, the 1½ cups water, and the quartered onion. Bring to a boil over high heat; reduce heat, cover, and simmer for 1 hour. Strain; discard neck, giblets, and seasonings. Return broth to pan; boil to reduce to ¼ cup. Set aside.

Siphon (or spoon out) and discard fat from roasting pan. Turn duckling breast up. Add whole onions and yams to pan, arranging them around or under rack; turn to coat with drippings. Continue to roast, turning vegetables several times, until yams are tender when pierced, onions give readily when gently squeezed, and meat near thighbone is no longer pink when slashed (45 to 60 more minutes).

Transfer duckling and vegetables to a platter and keep warm. Skim and discard fat from pan drippings, then add broth, slivered tangerine peel, tangerine juice, and honey. Stir together cornstarch and the 2 teaspoons water; stir into pan. Bring to a boil over high heat; then boil, stirring, until sauce is thickened (about 1 minute). Season to taste with salt and pepper. Pour into a bowl.

To serve, cut each onion in half. Cut duckling into quarters with poultry shears; garnish with strips of tangerine peel, if desired. Pass sauce at the table. Makes 2 or 3 servings.

Tea-smoked Duck

(Pictured on facing page)

Purchase steamed buns from an Oriental bakery, or use readily available brown-and-serve rolls.

> **4 to 5-pound duckling (thawed if frozen)**
> 1 **teaspoon salt**
> 1 **tablespoon Szechwan peppercorns**
> 2 **tablespoons dry sherry**
> ¼ **cup** *each* **rice, firmly packed brown sugar, and black tea leaves**
> 2 **tablespoons coarsely chopped orange peel**
> 6 **quarter-size slices fresh ginger, crushed**
> 5 **green onions (including tops)**
> 8 **to 12 plain steamed buns or 8 to 10 brown-and-serve rolls**
> **Hoisin sauce**
> **Fresh cilantro (coriander) sprigs**

Remove duckling neck and giblets; reserve for other uses, if desired. Discard lumps of fat. Rinse duckling inside and out and pat dry. With a fork, prick skin all over at 1-inch intervals.

In a small frying pan over medium-low heat, cook salt and peppercorns, shaking pan often, until salt begins to brown and peppercorns become fragrant (about 10 minutes). Let cool, then coarsely grind with a mortar and pestle or crush with a rolling pin. Combine peppercorn mixture with sherry; rub over duckling, inside and out.

To smoke duckling, you'll need a wok at least 14 inches in diameter (*do not* use an electric wok with a nonstick finish). Line wok with heavy-duty foil. Add rice, sugar, tea leaves, and orange peel; stir together. Position a round cake rack or steamer rack in bottom of wok, at least an inch above tea mixture. Set duckling, breast up, on rack; place wok over high heat.

When mixture begins to smoke, cover pan tightly and smoke for 5 minutes. Reduce heat to medium; continue to smoke, covered, for 15 more minutes. Turn off heat and leave covered until smoke subsides (about 15 more minutes). Remove duckling from wok; discard tea mixture. Place ginger and 2 of the onions inside body cavity; fasten opening shut with a small skewer. Place duckling, breast down, on a rack in a shallow roasting pan. Roast, uncovered, in a 375° oven for 1 hour.

Siphon (or spoon out) and discard fat from pan. Turn duckling over. Continue to roast until meat near thighbone is no longer pink when slashed (30 to 45 more minutes).

Remove duckling from oven. Siphon (or spoon out) all fat from pan. Increase oven temperature to 450°; return duckling to oven and continue to roast just until skin is crisp (about 5 more minutes).

Meanwhile, place each bun on a square of foil; arrange on a steaming rack or wire rack. Steam, covered, over simmering water until hot (about 5 minutes).

Slice duckling meat from bones; cut remaining 3 onions into thin slivers. To eat, place meat in a bun; add onions, hoisin, and cilantro, then close bun and eat out of hand. Makes 2 or 3 servings.

Roast Goose with Brandied Fruit Compote

Crisp, succulent roast goose, served with a spiced fruit compote, makes a splendid holiday entrée.

> **Brandied Fruit Compote (recipe follows)**
> **9 to 11-pound goose (thawed if frozen)**
> 1 *each* **lemon and orange, thinly sliced**

Prepare Brandied Fruit Compote; after stirring in brandy, cover and refrigerate as directed.

Remove goose neck and giblets; reserve for other uses, if desired. Discard lumps of fat. Rinse goose inside and out; pat dry. Place lemon and orange slices in cavities; truss both cavities (see page 65). Prick skin all over at 1-inch intervals.

Place goose, breast down, on a rack in a large, shallow roasting pan. Roast, uncovered, in a 400° oven for 1 hour. Every 30 minutes, siphon (or spoon out) and discard fat from pan. Turn goose breast up, reduce oven temperature to 325°, and continue to roast until meat near thighbone is no longer pink when slashed (1½ to 2 more hours). Continue to siphon (or spoon out) fat from pan every 30 minutes.

Reheat and thicken compote as directed. Let cool slightly; pass at the table. Makes 6 servings.

Brandied Fruit Compote. In a 3-quart pan, combine 2 cups **water**, ½ cup **orange juice**, 3 tablespoons **honey**, 1 teaspoon grated **orange peel**, 5 **whole allspice**, ¼ teaspoon **ground ginger**, and 1 **cinnamon stick** (about 2 inches long). Stir in ½ cup **raisins**; 1 small **apple**, thinly sliced; and 2 cups **mixed dried fruit**. Bring to a boil over high heat; reduce heat, cover, and simmer for 3 minutes. Remove from heat and stir in ½ cup **brandy** or orange juice. Let cool, then cover and refrigerate for at least 4 hours or until next day.

Stir together ½ cup of the fruit liquid and 1 tablespoon **cornstarch;** then stir into fruit. Cook over medium-high heat, stirring, until thickened.

Crackling-crisp skin is just one reason to enjoy Tea-smoked Duck (facing page). Orange peel and Szechwan spices season this Chinese treat, served tucked inside a fluffy steamed bun.

75

Versatile Cooked Poultry

Salads, casseroles, pastries & other bonuses

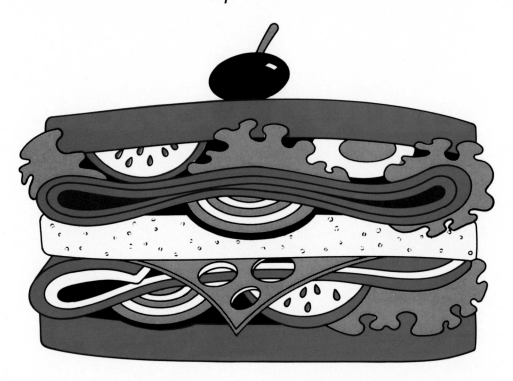

With cooked poultry as the starting point, you're on your way to an impressive variety of good-tasting dishes made in short order. Salads, soups, sandwiches, and casseroles, plus pastries, pasta, and crêpes—they're all well represented in this chapter. You'll find familiar favorites such as chef's salad, lasagne, and enchiladas, as well as a few more unusual entrées—Strawberry Chicken Salad Plates and Turkey with Italian Beans & Caviar, for example.

Any of these recipes would be an ideal way to use the leftovers from a holiday turkey or other bird. But these dishes are all so good that you may not want to wait until you have leftover meat to make them. One convenient

way to have cooked meat on hand for these recipes is simply to make more poultry than you need for one meal—fry or broil a few extra pieces, or roast two chickens instead of just one. For extra-moist cooked chicken breasts, try the steeping technique described on page 58. And if you have a microwave oven, you can use it to fix plain cooked chicken in no time (see the microwave feature on page 84).

Nearly all of the recipes in this chapter give you the option of using cooked chicken or turkey. If you're fortunate enough to have leftover meat from game hens, duck, goose, or another bird, you can use it as well. Plan on getting 3 to 4 cups meat from a whole 3 to 4-pound frying chicken, or about 1½ cups from a whole (1-pound) chicken breast.

Winter Chicken Salad

Though main-dish salads are most often associated with warmer days, they can be an especially welcome touch on a winter menu. This salad pairs chicken with two fruits available all year round—apples and tangy dried apricots.

    ⅓ cup chopped almonds
    ⅓ cup *each* fresh lemon juice and salad oil
    2 tablespoons *each* poppy seeds, honey,
       and Dijon mustard
    ½ teaspoon grated lemon peel
    ½ cup moist-pack dried apricots
    4 cups bite-size pieces cooked chicken or
       turkey
    1 medium-size red apple
    ¼ cup sliced green onion tops
       Salt
       Butter lettuce leaves

Spread almonds in a shallow baking pan and toast in a 350° oven until golden (about 8 minutes). Set aside.

In a medium-size bowl, stir together lemon juice, oil, poppy seeds, honey, mustard, and lemon peel. Add apricots and stir to coat, then cover and let stand for 30 minutes to 1 hour. Lift out apricots and set aside; stir chicken into dressing. (At this point, you may cover apricots and chicken mixture separately and refrigerate until next day.)

Core and thinly slice apple. Stir apple, onions, and almonds into chicken mixture; season to taste with salt. Line 4 individual plates with lettuce; mound about a fourth of the chicken salad in center of each. Garnish each serving with a fourth of the apricots. Makes 4 servings.

Strawberry Chicken Salad Plates

Strawberries, kiwi fruit, and poultry may sound like an unusual combination, but in fact, the tart-sweet fruits are a perfect complement to mild-flavored chicken or turkey. Serve these attractive salad plates for a carefree luncheon or brunch.

       Fruit Vinegar Dressing (recipe follows)
    4 cups bite-size pieces cooked chicken or
       turkey
       Butter lettuce leaves
    2 cups strawberries, halved
    1 or 2 kiwis, peeled and sliced

Prepare Fruit Vinegar Dressing; stir in chicken. Cover and let stand for 1 hour.

To serve, line 4 individual plates with lettuce; place about ½ cup of the strawberries on each. With a slotted spoon, lift chicken from dressing; place a fourth of the chicken on each plate alongside berries. Garnish with kiwi slices, then drizzle remaining dressing over fruit. Makes 4 servings.

Fruit Vinegar Dressing. In a large bowl, stir together ½ cup **salad oil**; ¼ cup **strawberry, raspberry,** or **cider vinegar**; 2 tablespoons **sugar**; ½ teaspoon *each* **paprika, salt,** and **dry mustard**; and 1 **green onion** (including top), finely chopped.

Mexican Chicken & Pasta Salad

Lively Mexican flavorings season a hearty salad of chicken, shell-shaped pasta, and Cheddar cheese. Serve it as a main dish for four diners, or as a satisfying side dish for six.

    8 ounces small shell macaroni
       Boiling salted water
    2 tablespoons salad oil
    ½ cup mayonnaise
    1 can (4 oz.) diced green chiles
    1 jar (4 oz.) diced pimentos, drained
    1 teaspoon *each* oregano leaves and
       cumin seeds
    2 teaspoons chili powder
    1 tablespoon white wine vinegar
    ½ cup chopped green onions
       (including tops)
    1 cup finely diced jicama or celery
    1½ cups bite-size pieces cooked chicken
       or turkey
    2 cups (8 oz.) shredded Cheddar cheese
    1 can (2¼ oz.) sliced ripe olives, drained
       Parsley or fresh cilantro (coriander)
       sprigs

Following package directions, cook macaroni in boiling salted water until *al dente*. Drain, rinse under cold running water, and drain again. Let cool.

In a large bowl, stir together oil, mayonnaise, chiles, pimentos, oregano, cumin seeds, chili powder, and vinegar. Add macaroni and stir to mix; then stir in onions, jicama, chicken, and cheese.

Spoon mixture into a serving bowl. Sprinkle olives over top, then garnish with parsley. If made ahead, cover and refrigerate until next day; serve at room temperature. Makes 4 to 6 servings.

This showy main-dish salad in an edible bowl looks striking at a springtime luncheon or supper. To serve, cut Chicken & Pea Pod Salad in a Pastry Bowl (facing page) into generous wedges.

Chicken & Pea Pod Salad in a Pastry Bowl

(Pictured on facing page)

Our spectacular entrée salad offers great contrasts in texture and flavor: a crackling-crisp, chewy crust topped with tender-crisp pea pods and cool, creamy chicken salad.

    Pastry Bowl (recipe follows)
 3 cups bite-size pieces cooked chicken or
    turkey
 1 can (8 oz.) water chestnuts, drained and
    sliced
 ½ cup thinly sliced green onions
    (including tops)
 2 hard-cooked eggs, coarsely chopped
 1 cup sour cream
 2 teaspoons *each* sugar and curry powder
 1 teaspoon lime juice
 ½ teaspoon ground ginger
    Salt and pepper
 ¼ pound Chinese pea pods (also called
    snow or sugar peas), ends and strings
    removed
    Fresh cilantro (coriander) sprigs

Prepare Pastry Bowl and set aside.

In a large bowl, combine chicken, water chestnuts, onions, and eggs. In a small bowl, stir together sour cream, sugar, curry powder, lime juice, and ginger. Pour dressing over chicken mixture; mix well, then season to taste with salt and pepper. (At this point, you may cover and refrigerate until next day.)

Drop pea pods into a 1½ to 2-quart pan of rapidly boiling water; boil, uncovered, for 1½ minutes. Drain, plunge into cold water, and drain again. Pat dry. Arrange pea pods over bottom and up sides of Pastry Bowl. Pile chicken salad on top and garnish with cilantro. Cut into wedges. Makes 4 to 6 servings.

Pastry Bowl. In a 1½ to 2-quart pan, combine ⅔ cup **water**, 5 tablespoons **butter** or margarine, and ¼ teaspoon **salt**. Bring to a boil over high heat; boil until butter is melted. Remove pan from heat and add ⅔ cup **all-purpose flour** all at once. Stir vigorously until smooth.

Reduce heat to medium. Return pan to heat. Cook, stirring rapidly, until dough forms a ball and leaves sides of pan (about 1 minute). Remove from heat; add 3 **eggs,** one at a time, beating after each addition until dough is smooth and glossy. Spread dough evenly over bottom and up sides of a greased 9-inch spring-form pan.

Bake in a 400° oven until puffy and browned (about 40 minutes). Turn off oven. With a wooden pick, pierce crust in 10 to 12 places and let dry in closed oven for about 10 minutes; then remove from oven, place on a rack, and let cool completely. Remove from pan.

If made ahead, cover loosely with foil and store at room temperature until next day. For longer storage, wrap cooled bowl airtight and freeze. Recrisp crust before using: heat cooled bowl (or fully thawed frozen bowl), uncovered, in a 400° oven for 10 minutes. Let cool on a rack before filling.

Make-ahead Chef's Salad

Chicken, bacon, fresh vegetables, and a creamy herb-mustard dressing add up to hearty salad that's perfect for a busy-day luncheon or dinner.

    6 cups shredded lettuce (iceberg,
       romaine, or a combination)
    3 medium-size carrots, shredded
    4 green onions (including tops), thinly
       sliced
    3 stalks celery, sliced
    3 cups shredded cooked chicken or
       turkey
    1 can (2¼ oz.) sliced ripe olives, drained
 1½ cups mayonnaise
    1 tablespoon Dijon mustard
    2 tablespoons minced mild red onion
    1 clove garlic, minced or pressed
    ¼ teaspoon *each* Italian herb seasoning
       and paprika
       Salt and pepper
    2 medium-size tomatoes
    2 hard-cooked eggs
    6 slices bacon, crisply cooked and
       crumbled
    2 tablespoons chopped parsley

Arrange lettuce in an even layer in a shallow 4-quart serving dish. Top with carrots, green onions, celery, chicken, and olives. In a small bowl, stir together mayonnaise, mustard, red onion, garlic, herb seasoning, and paprika. Season to taste with salt and pepper. Spread dressing evenly over chicken mixture, cover, and refrigerate for at least 2 hours or until next day.

Just before serving, cut tomatoes into wedges and slice eggs; decoratively arrange atop salad. Sprinkle with bacon and parsley. For each serving, scoop down to bottom of dish and lift out a portion of all layers. Makes about 6 servings.

Sesame Turkey Salad

This Oriental-style turkey salad gets its crunch from bean sprouts and toasted sesame seeds. The lemony dressing is flavored with hoisin sauce and sesame oil (both are available in well-stocked supermarkets and Asian markets).

    ⅓ cup sesame seeds
    4 cups shredded cooked turkey or chicken
    ½ cup thinly sliced green onions
       (including tops)
    3 cups bean sprouts (about ½ lb.)
    ½ cup chopped fresh cilantro (coriander)
    8 cups bite-size pieces romaine lettuce
       Hoisin-Lemon Dressing (recipe follows)

Toast sesame seeds in a wide frying pan over medium heat until golden (about 5 minutes), stirring frequently. Set aside.

In a 4-quart bowl, layer turkey, onions, bean sprouts, cilantro, and lettuce. (At this point, you may cover and refrigerate for up to 4 hours.)

Prepare Hoisin-Lemon Dressing. Pour dressing and sesame seeds over salad, then toss gently with 2 forks until ingredients are well combined. Makes about 4 servings.

Hoisin-Lemon Dressing. In a small bowl, combine ⅓ cup *each* **hoisin sauce** and **fresh lemon juice;** 1 teaspoon minced **fresh ginger;** 1 clove **garlic,** minced or pressed; and ¼ cup *each* **sesame oil** and **salad oil** (or ½ cup salad oil).

Turkey with Italian Beans & Caviar

White beans, inexpensive caviar, and a tangerine vinaigrette transform leftover turkey into an elegant, unusual main dish that goes together in minutes.

       Tangerine Vinaigrette (recipe follows)
    2 cans (about 16 oz. *each*) cannellini (white
       kidney beans) or 4 cups other canned or
       lightly seasoned cooked white beans
    3 cups bite-size pieces cooked turkey or
       chicken
    ⅓ cup minced onion
    1 jar (2 oz.) black or red whitefish or
       lumpfish caviar
       Salt and pepper

Prepare Tangerine Vinaigrette; set aside. Drain beans, rinse, and drain again; then add to vinaigrette along with turkey and onion. Toss until well combined.

Place caviar in a fine wire strainer. Rinse under cold running water until water runs clear; drain. Mix 1 tablespoon of the caviar into salad; season to taste with salt and pepper. Divide salad equally among 4 or 5 individual plates (or spoon onto a platter); garnish with remaining caviar. Makes 4 or 5 servings.

Tangerine Vinaigrette. In a large bowl, combine ⅓ cup **salad oil,** 3 tablespoons *each* **fresh lemon juice** and **tangerine juice,** and 1 teaspoon grated **tangerine peel.**

Curried Chicken Salad

Here's the dish to choose whenever a creamy, curry-flavored salad strikes your fancy. Like Winter Chicken Salad (page 77), it uses ingredients that are available any time of year. For a buffet-style meal, accompany the salad with an assortment of cheeses and marinated vegetables. You might also use it as a sandwich filling (try tucking it inside a crusty baguette).

    3   tablespoons sliced almonds
    ½   cup mayonnaise
    ½   teaspoon *each* garlic salt and prepared
        mustard
    1   teaspoon curry powder
    ⅛   teaspoon ground red pepper (cayenne)
    2   teaspoons lemon juice
    2   tablespoons finely chopped Major
        Grey's chutney
    3½ cups bite-size pieces cooked chicken or
        turkey
    ⅔   cup thinly sliced celery
    2   green onions (including tops), thinly
        sliced
    1   small apple, cored and diced

Spread almonds in a shallow baking pan and toast in a 350° oven until golden (about 8 minutes). Set aside.

In a large bowl, combine mayonnaise, garlic salt, mustard, curry powder, pepper, lemon juice, and chutney. Add chicken, celery, onions, and apple; stir to blend. If made ahead, cover and refrigerate until next day.

Just before serving, sprinkle with almonds. Makes about 4 servings.

Chicken-Artichoke Monte Cristos

Artichokes stand in for the traditional ham in our version of these tasty French-toasted sandwiches.

1½ cups shredded cooked chicken or turkey

1 jar (6 oz.) marinated artichoke hearts, drained and chopped

1 tablespoon *each* mayonnaise and dry sherry

¾ teaspoon dry rosemary

8 slices firm-textured white bread

4 square slices (1 oz. *each*) Swiss or jack cheese

2 eggs

¼ cup milk

About 2 tablespoons butter or margarine

In a bowl, stir together chicken, artichokes, mayonnaise, sherry, and rosemary until well combined. Spread chicken mixture evenly over 4 of the bread slices; top each with a slice of cheese, then with another slice of bread, pressing lightly to hold sandwiches together.

In a pie pan, beat eggs and milk until well blended. Melt about 1 tablespoon of the butter in a 10 to 12-inch frying pan over medium heat. Meanwhile, dip 2 of the sandwiches in egg mixture to coat both sides (hold sandwiches together firmly to prevent them from coming apart); drain briefly. Place in frying pan, cheese side down. Cook, turning once, until golden brown on both sides (about 5 minutes *total*). Remove from pan and keep warm. Repeat with remaining 2 sandwiches, adding more butter as needed. Serve immediately; eat with knife and fork. Makes 4 servings.

Chicken Supper Sandwiches

Buttery toasted English muffins are the foundations for these extra-easy hot chicken and tomato sandwiches.

4 slices bacon, cut in half crosswise

1½ cups sliced cooked chicken or turkey breast

2 English muffins, split, toasted, and buttered

4 slices mild red onion

1 large tomato, peeled and cut into 4 thick slices

½ cup shredded Cheddar cheese

In a wide frying pan, partially cook bacon over medium heat to remove most of fat (bacon should still be limp). Lift out and drain on paper towels.

Arrange chicken over muffin halves. Top each with an onion slice and a tomato slice, then sprinkle evenly with cheese. Arrange 2 bacon pieces atop each muffin half.

Place muffins in a rimmed baking pan. Broil about 6 inches below heat until cheese is bubbly and bacon is crisp (3 to 5 minutes). Serve sandwiches open-faced; eat with knife and fork. Makes 2 servings.

Savory Sandwich Loaf

Picnickers on the go will appreciate the convenience of our hollowed bread loaf filled with piquant chicken-ham salad. It tucks neatly into a knapsack or saddle bag, ready to be cut into thick slices for serving.

1 long loaf (1 lb.) French bread

2 cups finely chopped cooked chicken or turkey

2 cups finely chopped cooked ham (8 to 10 oz.)

4 hard-cooked eggs, chopped

⅓ cup finely chopped green onions (including tops)

1 cup finely chopped dill pickles, drained

½ cup chopped parsley

6 tablespoons mayonnaise

3 tablespoons drained capers

2 tablespoons Dijon mustard

1 teaspoon thyme leaves

2 teaspoons *each* vinegar and Worcestershire

Garlic salt and pepper

Cut 1½-inch-thick slices off both ends of bread; set aside. Using a long serrated knife and your fingers, cut and pull out soft center, leaving a shell about ½ inch thick. Set hollowed loaf aside; reserve soft bread from center for other uses, if desired.

In a bowl, combine chicken, ham, eggs, onions, pickles, and parsley. In another bowl, stir together mayonnaise, capers, mustard, thyme, vinegar, and Worcestershire. Stir into chicken mixture; season to taste with garlic salt and pepper.

Stand hollowed loaf on end and stuff with filling, using a long wooden spoon to pack tightly. Set end slices in place; wrap loaf in foil and refrigerate for at least 4 hours or until next day. To serve, cut into ¾-inch-thick slices. Makes 4 to 6 servings.

Chicken Crêpe Stack

It looks a little like a fancy layer cake, but our crêpe stack is really an unusual, savory sandwich. To make this impressive entrée, just stack paper-thin crêpes, thinly sliced chicken, fresh spinach leaves, jack cheese, and a nippy mustard dressing.

  Basic Crêpes (recipe follows)
  ¾ cup mayonnaise
  ¼ cup *each* thinly sliced green onions (including tops) and Dijon mustard
  ¼ pound spinach
  ½ to ¾ pound chicken or turkey, very thinly sliced (about 2½ cups small slices)
  12 ounces jack cheese, very thinly sliced

Prepare Basic Crêpes; set aside. In a small bowl, stir together mayonnaise, onions, and mustard; set aside. Remove and discard spinach stems and any tough center veins from leaves; rinse leaves well and pat dry. Set aside.

To assemble, place one crêpe in the middle of a serving board. Spread lightly with mayonnaise mixture, then arrange enough chicken on top to completely cover crêpe (use about ¼ of the chicken). Add another crêpe, spread lightly with mayonnaise mixture, and evenly cover with spinach leaves. Top with a third crêpe; spread with mayonnaise mixture and cover with cheese slices. Repeat spinach and cheese layers, then continue to stack crêpes, layering in this order: chicken, spinach, cheese, spinach, cheese. Top stack with the last plain crêpe (don't spread with mayonnaise mixture).

Cover and refrigerate crêpe stack for at least 4 hours or until next day. To serve, cut into wedges. Makes 6 to 8 servings.

Basic Crêpes. In a blender, whirl 1⅓ cups **milk,** 5 **eggs,** and ⅔ cup **all-purpose flour** until smooth.

Heat a 7 to 8-inch crêpe pan or other flat-bottomed frying pan over medium heat. For each crêpe, add ¼ teaspoon **butter** or margarine and swirl to coat surface. Stir batter, then pour 3 tablespoons of batter all at once into center of pan; swiftly tilt pan so batter flows over entire bottom of pan.

Cook until surface of crêpe is dry and edges are lightly browned (about 40 seconds). Run a small spatula around edges to loosen. Pick up crêpe with your fingertips and flip over. Cook second side for about 20 seconds (this side doesn't brown). Turn crêpe out of pan onto a plate. Repeat with remaining batter, stacking crêpes as made.

Use crêpes within a few hours. Or let stacked crêpes cool; then wrap airtight and refrigerate for 2 to 3 days, or freeze for longer storage. To avoid tearing, bring crêpes to room temperature before separating. Makes about 20 crêpes.

Chicken & Asparagus Crêpes

Here's a sure-fire hit for a company meal: creamy chicken, asparagus, and mushrooms enclosed in tender crêpes. For spur-of-the-moment entertaining, have the crêpes already assembled in the freezer (they can be baked without thawing).

  5 tablespoons butter or margarine
  1 small onion, chopped
  ¼ pound mushrooms, sliced
  3 tablespoons all-purpose flour
  ⅔ cup regular-strength chicken broth, homemade (page 53) or purchased
  ½ cup half-and-half (light cream) or milk
  3 cups bite-size pieces cooked chicken or turkey
  ⅓ cup grated Parmesan cheese
  ½ teaspoon dry rosemary
    Salt
  12 to 16 Basic Crêpes (recipe at left)
  12 to 16 cooked asparagus spears
  ¾ cup shredded Swiss cheese

Melt 2 tablespoons of the butter in a wide frying pan over medium heat. Add onion and mushrooms and cook, stirring occasionally, until onion is soft. Add remaining 3 tablespoons butter and flour; cook, stirring, until bubbly. Remove pan from heat. Gradually stir in broth and half-and-half. Return to heat; continue to cook, stirring, until sauce boils and thickens.

Remove from heat and stir in chicken, Parmesan cheese, and rosemary. Season to taste with salt; let cool slightly.

Spoon filling down center of each crêpe; then place an asparagus spear atop filling. Roll to enclose. Arrange crêpes, seam side down, in a shallow 9 by 13-inch casserole. (At this point, you may let cool, then cover and refrigerate until next day. Or freeze for up to 2 weeks: place filled crêpes, seam side down, on a greased baking sheet and freeze until firm, then wrap airtight and return to freezer.)

Bake, covered, in a 375° oven until heated through (about 20 minutes; about 30 minutes if refrigerated; 35 to 40 minutes if frozen). Uncover and sprinkle with Swiss cheese. Continue to bake, uncovered, until cheese is melted (about 5 more minutes). Makes 6 to 8 servings.

Tangy Chicken Noodle Soup

Yogurt adds tangy flavor and extra nutrition to a homey childhood treat.

- 2 tablespoons salad oil
- 1 large onion, chopped
- 6 cups regular-strength chicken broth, homemade (page 53) or purchased (one 49½-oz. can)
- 3 chicken bouillon cubes
- 3 cloves garlic, minced or pressed
- 1 teaspoon thyme leaves
- ¼ teaspoon *each* pepper and dill weed
- ¼ cup chopped parsley
- 3 small carrots, thinly sliced
- 6 ounces wide egg noodles
- 3 cups diced cooked chicken or turkey
- 2 cups plain yogurt
- 2 tablespoons cornstarch
  Sugar (optional)

Heat oil in a 5-quart pan over medium heat. Add onion and cook, stirring occasionally, until soft. Add broth, bouillon cubes, garlic, thyme, pepper, dill weed, parsley, and carrots. Bring to a boil over high heat; then reduce heat, cover, and simmer until carrots are tender to bite (about 10 minutes). Stir in noodles and cook, uncovered, until *al dente* (8 to 10 minutes). Stir in chicken.

Blend yogurt and cornstarch until smooth. Slowly stir into soup. Bring to a boil over high heat; then boil, stirring, until soup is slightly thickened. Taste; add a little sugar, if needed, to smooth flavor. Makes 4 to 6 servings.

Chicken Barley Soup

Anise seeds and orange segments give a fresh new look to an old-fashioned favorite.

- 3 tablespoons butter or margarine
- 1 large onion, thinly sliced
- 1 clove garlic, minced or pressed
- 6 cups regular-strength chicken broth, homemade (page 53) or purchased (one 49½-oz. can)
- ¼ cup pearl barley
- ⅛ teaspoon anise seeds
- 3 small carrots, thinly sliced
- 2 medium-size oranges
- 2 cups shredded cooked chicken or turkey

Melt butter in a 3 to 4-quart pan over medium heat. Add onion and garlic; cook, stirring, until onion is soft. Add broth, barley, and anise seeds. Bring to a boil over high heat; reduce heat, cover, and simmer until barley is tender to bite (about 30 minutes). Add carrots; cover and continue to simmer until carrots are tender to bite (about 10 more minutes).

Grate enough peel from one orange to make ¼ teaspoon; set aside. Then cut all remaining peel and white membrane from oranges; cut segments free and add to soup with reserved orange peel and chicken. Cover and simmer until chicken is hot (about 5 more minutes). Makes 4 servings.

Russian Spinach Soup

San Francisco's Russian bakery-delicatessens sometimes feature a spinach soup like this one, laden with vegetables and chunks of chicken.

- 1¼ to 1½ pounds spinach
- 1 cup sour cream
- ½ teaspoon dill weed
- 9½ cups regular-strength chicken broth, homemade (page 53) or purchased (one 49½-oz. can plus two 14½-oz. cans)
- 2 large thin-skinned potatoes
- 2 large carrots, shredded
- 2 large green bell peppers, seeded and diced
- 2 stalks celery, sliced
- 4 green onions (including tops), cut into 1-inch lengths
- 5 cups bite-size pieces cooked chicken or turkey
  Salt and pepper
- 4 hard-cooked eggs, coarsely chopped

Remove and discard spinach stems. Rinse leaves well; then drain, stack, and cut crosswise into strips. Set aside. Stir together sour cream and dill weed; set aside.

In an 8 to 10-quart pan, bring broth to a boil over medium heat. Meanwhile, dice potatoes. Add potatoes, carrots, bell peppers, celery, and onions to boiling broth. Return to a boil; then reduce heat, cover and simmer until potatoes are tender to bite (about 8 minutes).

Increase heat to high. Add spinach and chicken to pan; cook, uncovered, until soup returns to a boil. Season to taste with salt and pepper. At the table, pass eggs and sour cream-dill mixture to spoon into individual portions. Makes 8 to 10 servings.

Microwave
Tips & Techniques

Microwaving is the fastest way to defrost chicken; to cook poultry for salads, sandwiches, and other recipes; and to make tasty entrées.

NOTE: We developed these recipes using a 650-watt microwave oven and four power designations: **HIGH (100%)**—600 to 650 watts; **MEDIUM-HIGH (70%)**—450 to 490 watts; **MEDIUM (50%)**—300 to 350 watts; and **MEDIUM-LOW (30%)**—180 to 210 watts. But since cooking power of microwave ovens varies with the manufacturer, use our cooking times only as general guides. Always test for doneness after the minimum time given; be sure to allow for standing time.

Defrosting

To defrost, use **MEDIUM (50%)** power, and cover chicken with plastic wrap or wax paper. (See also "Defrosting tips," at right.)

Type of Chicken/Weight	Defrosting Instructions
Whole, 3½ lbs.	Microwave 10 minutes; let stand 10 minutes. Repeat. Microwave 5 minutes; let stand 5 minutes. Set aside neck and giblets for other uses. Microwave 2 minutes.
Cut up, 3½ lbs.	Microwave 10 minutes; let stand 10 minutes. Repeat. Reserve neck and giblets for other uses; set aside wings (they should be thawed). Arrange remaining pieces in a single layer. Microwave 5 minutes; let stand 5 minutes. Microwave 2 minutes.
Whole legs (2), thighs attached (1 lb. *total*)	Microwave 5 minutes; let stand 5 minutes. Microwave 4 minutes; let stand 4 minutes. Microwave 1 minute longer, if necessary.
Whole breast (1), split (1 lb.)	Microwave 5 minutes; let stand 5 minutes. Microwave 3 minutes; let stand 3 minutes. Microwave 1 minute longer, if necessary.

Defrosting tips. Place chicken on a microwave-proof platter. Halfway through each microwaving period, turn chicken over and rotate platter a quarter turn. As soon as possible, separate pieces, arranging them with meatiest portions to outside.

After defrosting, meat should be flexible but still very cold. (Defrosting times will vary for birds of weights other than those given in chart.)

Cooking Techniques

Chicken cooked in the microwave doesn't turn golden brown and crisp as it would in a frying pan or conventional oven. If you want chicken with a rich brown color, brush the surface with a mixture of two parts of melted butter or water to one part of brown gravy sauce. You can also color the skin by rubbing it with soy sauce or with a mixture of paprika and butter.

Salt tends to draw moisture out of meat; this can interfere with the microwave cooking pattern. For best results, wait until chicken is completely cooked before salting it.

If excess liquid accumulates in the bottom of the cooking container, it will absorb microwaves and decrease cooking efficiency. You may need to siphon or spoon out liquid occasionally during cooking.

Remember to rotate whole birds and chicken pieces during cooking so meat cooks evenly. Cook for the minimum time given; before testing for doneness, let chicken stand, covered, for 5 minutes (or follow recipe directions). Meat near bone should no longer be pink when slashed. If chicken is not done, microwave it further, in 30-second increments.

Whole frying chicken. Remove neck and giblets; reserve for other uses, if desired. Discard lumps of fat. Rinse chicken inside and out, then pat dry.

Stuff, if desired—see pages 64 and 65 for suggestions. (Close stuffed cavities with string and wooden picks—*not metal skewers.*) Place, breast down, on a nonmetallic rack in a 7 by 11-inch microwave-proof baking dish. Cover with heavy-duty plastic wrap or wax paper.

For a 3 to 3½-pound bird, microwave on **HIGH (100%)** for 6 to 7 minutes per pound, turning chicken over and rotating dish a quarter turn halfway through cooking.

Cut-up frying chicken. Reserve neck and giblets for other uses, if desired. Rinse chicken and pat dry. In a 7 by 11-inch microwave-proof baking dish, arrange chicken pieces, skin side down, with meaty portions to outside of dish. Cover with heavy-duty plastic wrap or wax paper. For a 3 to 3½-pound bird, microwave on **HIGH (100%)** for 6 to 7 minutes per pound, turning pieces skin side up and rotating dish a quarter turn halfway through cooking.

Chicken breast, split. Rinse chicken and pat dry. Skin and bone, if desired. Place chicken in a 9-inch microwave-proof baking dish. Cover with heavy-duty plastic wrap or wax paper.

For a 1-pound breast, microwave on **HIGH (100%)** for 4 to 5 minutes, turning chicken over and rotating dish a quarter turn halfway through cooking.

Whole chicken legs, thighs attached. Rinse and pat dry. In a 7 by 11-inch microwave-proof baking dish, arrange chicken pieces, skin side down, with thighs to outside of dish and drumsticks to center. Cover with heavy-duty plastic wrap or wax paper.

For 2 chicken legs with thighs attached (about 1 lb. *total*), microwave on **HIGH (100%)** for 7 minutes, turning pieces skin side up and rotating dish a quarter turn halfway through cooking.

Teriyaki Ginger Chicken Breast

This boned chicken breast marinates for an hour with ginger and soy, then cooks in minutes in the microwave. For a low-calorie meal, round out the menu with steamed vegetables and hot rice.

1 whole chicken breast (about 1 lb.), skinned, boned, and split (see page 93)
3 tablespoons soy sauce
1 tablespoon *each* sugar and dry sherry
½ teaspoon grated fresh ginger
1 clove garlic, minced or pressed
Fresh cilantro (coriander) sprigs

Rinse chicken, pat dry, and set aside. In a 9-inch microwave-proof baking dish, stir together soy, sugar, sherry, ginger, and garlic. Add chicken and turn to coat with marinade. Cover and let stand for 1 hour, turning chicken over after 30 minutes.

Drain and reserve marinade from chicken. Cover dish with heavy-duty plastic wrap or wax paper and microwave on **HIGH (100%)** for 3 minutes. Rotate dish a quarter turn. Turn chicken over and brush with marinade; re-cover and microwave on **HIGH (100%)** for 2 more minutes. Let stand for 3 minutes. Meat in thickest part should no longer be pink when slashed. Garnish with cilantro. Makes 2 servings.

Sweet Chili Chicken

Chili sauce and a hint of vinegar and sugar give chicken a tangy, slightly sweet flavor.

2 chicken legs, thighs attached (about 1 lb. *total*), skinned
½ cup tomato-based chili sauce
1 tablespoon *each* distilled white vinegar, brown sugar, and minced green onion (including top)
½ teaspoon *each* dry mustard and Worcestershire

Rinse chicken and pat dry; set aside. In a 9-inch microwave-proof baking dish, stir together chili sauce, vinegar, sugar, onion, mustard, and Worcestershire. Add chicken and turn to coat, then arrange with thighs toward outside of dish. Cover with heavy-duty plastic wrap and microwave on **HIGH (100%)** for 5 minutes. Let stand, covered, for 5 minutes. Rotate dish a quarter turn and turn pieces over. Spoon sauce over top and microwave, uncovered, on **HIGH (100%)** for 3 more minutes or until sauce is thickened. Let stand, uncovered, for 3 to 5 minutes. Meat near thighbone should no longer be pink when slashed. Makes 2 servings.

Chicken Soup with Parmesan Cream

Egg yolks, Parmesan, and cream enrich this velvety-smooth soup.

2 tablespoons butter or margarine
2 medium-size carrots, thinly sliced
2 stalks celery, thinly sliced
1 medium-size onion, thinly sliced
   About ⅓ cup chopped parsley
   Parmesan Cream (recipe follows)
6 cups regular-strength chicken broth, homemade (page 53) or purchased (one 49½-oz. can)
3 cups bite-size pieces cooked chicken or turkey
½ teaspoon thyme leaves
2 tablespoons *each* cornstarch and water
   Salt and pepper
   Freshly grated Parmesan cheese

Melt butter in a 4 to 5-quart pan over medium heat. Add carrots, celery, onion, and ¼ cup of the parsley; cook, stirring occasionally, until carrots are tender to bite (about 15 minutes). Meanwhile, prepare Parmesan Cream; set aside.

Add broth, chicken, and thyme to carrot mixture. Bring to a boil over high heat; then reduce heat, cover, and simmer for 5 minutes. Stir together cornstarch and water; stir into broth mixture and cook, stirring, until slightly thickened.

Stir about 1 cup of the hot soup into Parmesan Cream, then return all to pan. Reduce heat to low and cook, stirring, just until heated through (*do not boil* or soup will curdle). Season to taste with salt and pepper. Sprinkle soup with remaining parsley; pass cheese at the table to add to each portion. Makes about 4 servings.

Parmesan Cream. In a bowl, beat 6 **egg yolks** until blended; then stir in 3 ounces **Parmesan cheese**, grated, and ½ cup **whipping cream.**

Turkey & Chile Soup

Whether you're watching from the grandstand or your favorite armchair, a mug of turkey soup with tomatoes, green chiles, and rice is just the thing for a football game on a blustery day. (If you transport the soup, either omit the tortilla strips or wrap them carefully in foil to avoid breakage.)

   Tortilla Strips (recipe follows)
1 can (16 oz.) tomatoes
1 large can (7 oz.) diced green chiles
1 small onion, cut into chunks
3 cups regular-strength chicken broth, homemade (page 53) or purchased (about two 14½-oz. cans)
3 cups bite-size pieces cooked turkey or chicken
2 cups cooked brown rice
1 package (10 oz.) frozen whole kernel corn, thawed
¾ teaspoon ground cumin
½ teaspoon garlic salt
¼ teaspoon chili powder
   Sour cream
   Fresh cilantro (coriander) leaves

Prepare Tortilla Strips; set aside. In a blender or food processor, combine tomatoes and their liquid, chiles, and onion; whirl until smooth. Pour into a 4-quart pan, add broth, and bring to a boil over high heat. Add turkey, rice, corn, cumin, garlic salt, and chili powder; reduce heat and simmer until heated through.

At the table, pass sour cream, cilantro, and Tortilla Strips to add to individual portions. Makes 4 to 6 servings.

Tortilla Strips. Cut 8 **flour tortillas** (each about 8 inches in diameter) into 1-inch-wide strips. Pour ½ cup **salad oil** into a wide frying pan over medium heat. When oil is hot enough to form ripples when pan is tilted, add tortilla strips, a few at a time; cook, turning, until golden. Drain on paper towels and keep warm in oven at lowest setting.

Post-holiday Turkey Chowder

Here's a great way to use up every last bit of a holiday bird. First make a rich, flavorful stock with the roast turkey carcass; then add yams, corn, and a generous quantity of cooked meat for a hearty soup.

   Turkey Stock (recipe follows)
2 tablespoons butter or margarine
1 large onion, chopped
1½ pounds yams or sweet potatoes, peeled and cut into ½-inch cubes
1 package (10 oz.) frozen whole kernel corn, thawed
3 to 4 cups bite-size pieces cooked turkey
   Salt and pepper
   Snipped chives or green onion tops

Prepare stock; set aside. Melt butter in a 5 to 6-quart pan over medium-high heat; add onion and yams and cook, stirring, until onion is soft.

Add stock to pan; bring to a boil over high heat. Reduce heat, cover, and simmer until yams are very soft (about 20 minutes). Add corn and turkey, cover, and simmer until turkey is hot (about 5 more minutes). Season to taste with salt and pepper; garnish with chives. Makes 6 to 8 servings.

Turkey Stock. Pull meat off a **roasted turkey carcass;** tear or cut into bite-size pieces and reserve to use in chowder. Break carcass to fit into a 6 to 8-quart pan. Add 1 **onion,** cut into chunks; 2 stalks **celery,** cut into chunks; 1 teaspoon *each* **rubbed sage** and **ground allspice;** 2 teaspoons **poultry seasoning;** 4 **chicken bouillon cubes;** 8 cups **water;** and 1 cup **whipping cream** (or 1 more cup water).

Bring to a boil over high heat; reduce heat, cover, and simmer for 2 hours. Strain stock; discard bones and vegetables. Skim and discard fat. If made ahead, let cool; then cover and refrigerate for up to 2 days. Makes about 8 cups.

Chicken Lasagne

Unlike its traditional tomato-based counterpart, this lasagne has a creamy wine and tarragon sauce.

- ½ **cup (¼ lb.) butter or margarine**
- 1 **pound mushrooms, sliced**
- ½ **cup dry white wine**
- ½ **teaspoon dry tarragon**
- ¼ **cup all-purpose flour**
- ¼ **teaspoon** *each* **white pepper and ground nutmeg**
- 2 **cups half-and-half (light cream)**
- 2 **cups regular-strength chicken broth, homemade (page 53) or purchased (about one 14½ oz. can)**
  Salt
- 12 **to 15 lasagne noodles**
  Boiling salted water
- 5 **cups shredded cooked chicken or turkey**
- 3 **cups (12 oz.) shredded Swiss cheese**

Melt ¼ cup of the butter in a wide frying pan over medium-high heat. Add mushrooms and cook, stirring, until soft. Add wine and tarragon, reduce heat to medium, and cook until almost all liquid has evaporated. Set aside.

Melt remaining ¼ cup butter in a 2-quart pan over medium heat. Blend in flour, pepper, and nutmeg; cook, stirring, until bubbly. Remove pan from

heat and gradually stir in half-and-half and broth. Return pan to heat; cook, stirring, until thickened. Stir in mushroom mixture. Season to taste with salt.

Cook noodles in a large quantity of boiling salted water until *al dente* (about 10 minutes). Drain, rinse under cold water, and drain again.

Spread a thin layer of sauce over bottom of a greased 9 by 13-inch baking dish. Arrange ⅓ of the noodles evenly over sauce; top with ⅓ of the chicken, ⅓ of the remaining sauce, and 1 cup of the cheese. Repeat layering 2 more times, ending with cheese. (At this point, you may let cool, then cover and refrigerate until next day.)

Bake, uncovered, in a 350° oven until hot and bubbly (about 40 minutes; about 50 minutes if refrigerated). Cut into squares. Makes 8 servings.

Curried Turkey over Rice

A sherried curry sauce and an array of condiments give leftover turkey a new look.

- ¼ **cup butter or margarine**
- 1 **large onion, chopped**
- 2 **cloves garlic, minced or pressed**
- 3 **tablespoons curry powder**
- ¼ **cup all-purpose flour**
- 2 **cups milk**
- ⅛ **teaspoon ground red pepper (cayenne)**
- ⅓ **cup dry sherry**
- 3 **to 4 cups bite-size pieces cooked turkey or chicken**
  Salt
  Hot cooked rice
  Condiments (suggestions follow)

Melt butter in a 4 to 5-quart pan over medium heat. Add onion and garlic and cook, stirring occasionally, until onion is soft. Add curry powder and cook, stirring, for 2 minutes. Add flour and cook, stirring, until bubbly. Remove pan from heat and gradually stir in milk. Return to heat and cook, stirring, until sauce boils and thickens. Blend in pepper and sherry. Add turkey and stir until heated through. Season to taste with salt.

Serve curry over rice; pass condiments at the table to add to each serving. Makes 4 servings.

Condiments. Choose 3 or 4 of the following (use ⅓ to ½ cup of each): Chopped **salted peanuts; Major Grey's chutney;** thinly sliced **green onions** (including tops); **raisins;** crisply cooked, crumbled **bacon; shredded coconut;** and chopped **hard-cooked eggs.**

Turkey in Mole Sauce

Chocolate is the secret to the rich flavor and color of Mexico's famous *mole* sauce.

- 3 tablespoons butter or margarine
- 1 large onion, chopped
- 2 cloves garlic, minced or pressed
- 3 tablespoons chili powder
- ¾ teaspoon *each* ground cinnamon and cloves
- 2¾ cups regular-strength chicken broth, homemade (page 53) or purchased
- 1 corn tortilla (6 to 7 inches in diameter), torn into pieces
- ¼ cup *each* sesame seeds and raisins
  Ground red pepper (cayenne)
- 2 ounces semisweet chocolate
  Guacamole (recipe follows)
- 24 flour tortillas (*each* about 8 inches in diameter) or corn tortillas (*each* 6 to 7 inches in diameter)
- 6 cups cooked turkey or chicken, in ½ by 2-inch strips
  Salt
- ¼ cup chopped fresh cilantro (coriander)

Melt butter in a 12 to 14-inch frying pan over medium heat; add onion and garlic and cook, stirring, until onion is soft. Stir in chili powder, cinnamon, and cloves; cook until bubbly. Gradually blend in 1 cup of the broth. Transfer to a blender or food processor; add tortilla pieces, sesame seeds, and raisins. Whirl until smoothly puréed, stopping and stirring often. Season to taste with pepper.

Return mole mixture to frying pan over medium heat; gradually add remaining 1¾ cups broth, stirring until well blended. Cook, stirring, until mixture comes to a simmer. Remove from heat; add chocolate and stir until melted.

Prepare Guacamole and set aside. Divide tortillas into 2 stacks; wrap each stack in foil. Heat in a 375° oven until hot (about 10 minutes).

Meanwhile, stir turkey into mole sauce. Cook over medium heat, stirring occasionally, until hot and thick. Season to taste with salt; then transfer to a serving dish and garnish with cilantro.

To serve, let diners spoon turkey mole and Guacamole into warm tortillas. Makes 12 servings.

Guacamole. Pit and peel 2 medium-size **avocados**; scoop pulp into a bowl and mash with a fork. Add 1 to 2 tablespoons **lemon juice**; ¼ cup chopped **fresh cilantro** (coriander); and 1 large **tomato,** peeled, seeded, and chopped. Season to taste with **salt** and **liquid hot pepper seasoning.**

Enchiladas with Tomatillo Sauce

Tart, fruity tomatillos, blended with green chiles and lime juice, give a refreshing character to the sauce for these make-ahead chicken enchiladas. Look for canned tomatillos in markets well stocked with Mexican products.

  Tomatillo Sauce (recipe follows)
  Chicken Filling (recipe on facing page)
  Salad oil
- 12 corn tortillas (*each* 6 to 7 inches in diameter)
- 2 cups (8 oz.) shredded jack cheese
- 2 cups finely shredded lettuce
- ½ cup sour cream
- 1 lime, thinly sliced
- ⅓ cup fresh cilantro (coriander) leaves
- ½ cup grated Parmesan cheese

Prepare Tomatillo Sauce, then Chicken Filling; set both aside.

Heat ½ inch of oil in a medium-size frying pan over medium-high heat until oil ripples when pan is tilted. Add one tortilla; cook, turning once, until tortilla just begins to brown (about 5 seconds per side). Lift out and lay flat on paper towels; while hot, spoon about ½ cup Chicken Filling down center. Roll to enclose. Lay filled tortilla, seam side down, in a 10 by 15-inch rimmed baking pan. Repeat with remaining tortillas and filling. (At this point, you may let cool, then cover and refrigerate enchiladas and Tomatillo Sauce separately until next day.)

Cover baking dish with foil, then bake enchiladas in a 350° oven until hot (about 15 minutes; about 30 minutes if refrigerated). Uncover and top with jack cheese. Continue to bake, uncovered, until cheese is melted (about 10 more minutes).

Meanwhile, reheat Tomatillo Sauce until simmering. To serve, spoon about ¾ cup of the sauce onto each of 6 individual plates. Then set 2 enchiladas atop sauce on each plate. Top each serving with about a sixth of the lettuce, sour cream, and lime slices; sprinkle with cilantro. Pass Parmesan cheese at the table to top individual servings. Makes 6 servings.

Tomatillo Sauce. Heat 6 tablespoons **salad oil** in a 3 to 4-quart pan over medium-high heat. Add 2 medium-size **onions,** chopped; cook, stirring, until onions are soft. Stir in 1 large can (7 oz.) **diced green chiles;** 2 cans (13 oz. *each*) **tomatillos,** drained; 1 cup **regular-strength chicken broth,** homemade (page 53) or purchased; 3 tablespoons **lime juice;** 2 teaspoons *each* **oregano leaves** and **sugar;** and

1 teaspoon **ground cumin.** Bring to a boil over high heat; then reduce heat to low and simmer, uncovered, for 25 minutes. Transfer mixture to a blender or food processor and whirl until smooth. Season to taste with **salt.**

Chicken Filling. In a large bowl, combine 4 cups coarsely shredded **cooked chicken** or turkey, 2 cups (8 oz.) shredded **jack cheese,** 1 large can (7 oz.) **diced green chiles,** and 1½ teaspoons **oregano leaves.** Season to taste with **salt.**

Individual Turkey-Vegetable Casseroles

Use your favorite pastry for the crust of these little deep-dish pies.

- ¼ **cup butter or margarine**
- 2 **medium-size onions, finely chopped**
- ½ **pound mushrooms, thinly sliced**
- 3 **tablespoons all-purpose flour**
- ¼ **teaspoon** *each* **pepper and dry rosemary**
- 1¼ **cups regular-strength chicken broth, homemade (page 53) or purchased**
- ½ **cup whipping cream**
- 1 **package (10 oz.) frozen peas and carrots, thawed**
- 2½ **to 3 cups bite-size pieces cooked turkey or chicken**
- 2 **tablespoons dry sherry (optional) Salt**
   Pastry for a double-crust 9-inch pie
- 1 **egg yolk beaten with 1 tablespoon water**

Melt butter in a wide frying pan over medium heat. Add onions and mushrooms and cook, stirring occasionally, until onions are soft. Stir in flour, pepper, and rosemary; cook until bubbly. Remove pan from heat; gradually stir in broth and cream. Return to heat and cook, stirring, until sauce boils and thickens. Stir in peas and carrots, turkey, and, if desired, sherry. Season to taste with salt.

Spoon turkey mixture into 4 individual 2-cup casseroles. (At this point, you may let cool, then cover and refrigerate until next day.)

Divide pastry into 4 equal portions. On a lightly floured board, roll out each portion to a circle 1½ to 2 inches greater in diameter than the diameter of casseroles. Cut a few slashes in each circle; or, if desired, use a small cookie cutter to cut out a design in center of each circle. Fit pastry over casseroles, pinch dough to casserole to seal, and crimp edges. Brush egg yolk mixture over pastry.

Bake in a 425° oven until pastry is golden brown and filling is bubbly (20 to 25 minutes). Check casseroles after 10 minutes; if edges are browning too quickly, protect with foil. Makes 4 servings.

Pasta with Mediterranean Chicken Sauce

Ingredients typical of Mediterranean cooking—tomatoes, zucchini, olive oil, pine nuts, and garlic—make a pasta sauce full of *buongusto.*

- 3 **to 4 tablespoons olive oil or salad oil**
- ¼ **cup pine nuts**
- 1 **large onion, chopped**
- 2 **cloves garlic, minced or pressed**
- 1½ **teaspoons** *each* **dry basil and oregano leaves**
- ¼ **to ½ teaspoon crushed red pepper**
- 2 **small zucchini, ends trimmed, cut into ⅛-inch-thick slices**
- ½ **pound mushrooms, sliced**
- 2 **medium-size tomatoes, cored and chopped**
- 1 **cup shredded cooked chicken or turkey**
- 10 **ounces fresh or dried fettuccine**
   Boiling salted water
   About ¾ cup grated Parmesan or Romano cheese
   Salt and pepper

Heat 2 tablespoons of the oil in a 12 to 14-inch frying pan over medium-high heat. Add pine nuts and cook, stirring, until lightly toasted (about 1 minute). With a slotted spoon, lift nuts from pan; set aside.

Add onion, garlic, basil, oregano, and pepper to pan. Cook, stirring occasionally, until onion is soft. Add 1 to 2 more tablespoons oil if needed to prevent sticking; then add zucchini, mushrooms, and tomatoes. Cook, stirring, for 3 minutes. Add chicken and stir just until hot (about 1 more minute).

Meanwhile, cook fettuccine in 4 to 6 quarts boiling salted water just until *al dente* (about 2 minutes for fresh pasta, about 8 minutes for dried pasta).

Drain pasta and pour onto a rimmed platter. Spoon chicken mixture over pasta and toss gently to mix. Sprinkle with pine nuts and ¼ cup of the cheese. At the table, pass remaining cheese, salt, and pepper to season individual servings. Makes 3 or 4 servings.

Poultry Pointers

Basic techniques for chicken & other birds

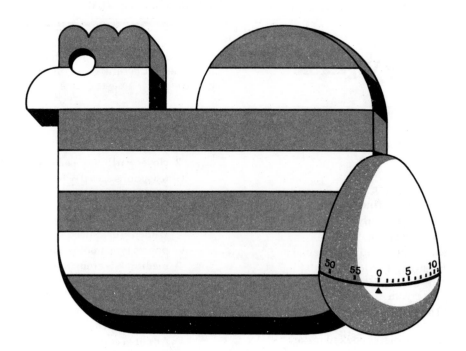

Star attraction at company meals and everyday dinners alike, poultry takes top honors for all-around reliable goodness. Few foods offer such richness of flavor as do chicken, turkey, duck, goose, and the smaller birds—quail, squab, pheasant, chukar, and game hen. In addition, all these birds are high in protein; and most are low in cholesterol and calories, inexpensive, and readily available.

Chicken is doubtless the most popular poultry today—it's sold everywhere, in every season. Thanks to improved methods of breeding, packaging, transport, and storage, it's also low in cost and consistently high in quality. Chicken appeals to today's cooks for its versatility, too; you can serve it simply roasted or fried, elaborately sauced, hot or cold, in soups, salads, sandwiches, or casseroles.

Whether you're an old hand at cooking poultry or a beginner, you'll find this chapter a handy reference guide to all the important poultry "basics." Look here for tips on purchasing, storing, thawing, handling, and checking for doneness. You'll also find step-by-step illustrations showing how to carve a roast turkey, bone a chicken breast, and disjoint, halve, and quarter a whole chicken. For thrifty cooks, mastering basic cutting and boning techniques is well worth the effort; though cut-up chickens are undeniably convenient, whole birds are still the best buy.

A French knife is a good choice for just about every poultry cutting task, though you can use poultry shears for halving and quartering chickens if you wish. Two other types of knives are also helpful tools. A *boning knife* has a narrow, curved blade that's specially designed to separate meat neatly from bones and skin. For easier carving, consider a *carving knife;* its long, flexible blade readily produces thin, attractive slices.

Types of Poultry

Frying chickens. Also called broilers and broiler-fryers, these are the perfect all-purpose birds—suitable not only for broiling and frying, but for roasting, baking, simmering, steaming, poaching, and barbecuing as well. Frying chickens are sold whole, cut up, and in parts—drumsticks, thighs, whole legs, breasts (boned or bone-in), and wings.

Frying chickens average 3 to 4 pounds, though weights may run as low as 2½ pounds or as high as 4½ pounds. By definition, these birds are 7 weeks old.

Roasting chickens. Roasting chickens—also known as young roasters—typically weigh 5 to 6 pounds, though some are as heavy as 8 pounds. Because of their size, these birds look almost as impressive as a turkey. They're a good choice when you're serving dinner for six, since each yields about 7 servings. Roasters are usually about 9 weeks old.

Stewing hens. Older and less tender than frying and roasting chickens, 3 to 5-pound stewing hens (or "heavy hens") are also much less available in retail markets. These birds are best used in slow-cooked soups and stews—long, slow simmering tenderizes them and brings out their rich flavor.

Rock Cornish game hens. These small (1 to 1½ lbs.), delicately flavored birds are a hybrid developed from the Cornish breed of chicken. Smaller game hens can be served one to a diner; larger ones make two servings. Game hens are usually 4 to 5 weeks old.

Turkeys. Choose between hen turkeys, averaging 8 to 15 pounds, and tom turkeys, averaging 16 to 24 pounds. During holiday time, you can find even larger toms, some as heavy as 30 pounds. Size has no bearing on tenderness or flavor, but it does affect the ratio of meat to bone. As a general rule, heavier birds have a higher proportion of meat to bone (and are thus a more economical purchase).

In addition to whole turkeys, most markets offer a variety of turkey parts. You'll find drumsticks, thighs, wings, and various cuts of breast meat—half or whole breasts, fillets, and boneless thinly sliced meat.

Ducks. Many varieties of duck are raised domestically; the most common one, Pekin, is what you'll find in grocery stores. These birds are usually labeled simply "duckling," and weigh 4 to 5 pounds. They're readily available frozen; some stores also offer them fresh.

Cutting Up a Chicken

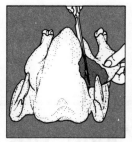 

Left: Place chicken breast up. Pull each leg away from body; cut through skin and meat, exposing joint. Bend thigh down; cut through joint. **Right:** Cut each leg between thigh and drumstick to joint. Bend pieces back to expose joint; sever.

 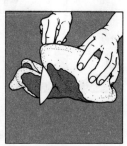

Left: Turn chicken over. Pull each wing away from body. Cut through skin and meat to expose joint; sever. **Right:** Turn breast up. To remove lower back, cut along bottom ribs on each side of breast to backbone. Bend back in half; cut to separate.

 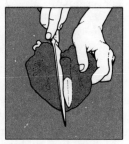

Left: With breast down, cut to shoulder joints along sides of upper back. Bend breast and back apart to expose joints; sever. **Right:** To halve breast, cut through thin membrane to keel bone; then cut to one side of bone and cartilage.

Geese. Like ducks, domestic geese are generally sold frozen, though you may be able to buy fresh birds during the holiday season. Fresh or frozen, geese are often a special-order item—so unless you live near a supplier carrying frozen birds in stock all year round, you'll need to plan in advance whenever you want to serve goose.

Geese are usually marketed in three basic sizes. The smallest birds weigh 8 to 10 pounds; medium-size birds weigh 10 to 12 pounds, while large ones average 12 to 14 pounds.

Halving & Quartering a Chicken

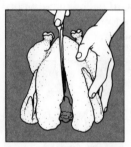 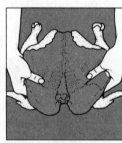

Left: To halve chicken, place bird breast up. Cut through meat and skin along entire length of breast, cutting to one side of keel bone (dark spoon-shaped bone). **Right:** Turn chicken skin side down. Then grasp both sides of breast and pull apart to flatten chicken.

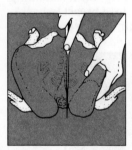 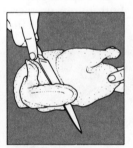

Left: Cut along entire length of back to one side of backbone. **Right:** To quarter chicken, first cut bird in half as directed above (first three drawings). Then divide each half into leg and wing portions. Holding knife at an angle, cut between thigh and breast, starting at backbone. Complete separation, following curve of leg with knife.

Specialty birds. The availability of farm-raised specialty birds is increasing, since they're now being produced in greater numbers. You'll find them fresh and frozen, in specialty food stores and even in some grocery stores. In certain parts of the country, though, you'll need to order the birds through service meat markets or directly from game farms. Check listings under "Poultry" and "Game" in the Yellow Pages of the telephone directory; some game farms also advertise in cooking magazines.

Quail, weighing just 3 to 6 ounces each, are perhaps the most widely available specialty bird. **Squab** (young pigeons) are fairly available; they weigh ¾ to 1 pound each. **Pheasant** (1½ to 3 lbs. each) and **chukar** (partridge, ¾ to 1 lb. each) are very seasonal; they're marketed primarily from late summer through autumn.

Number of servings. In general, you can figure the number of servings by a bird's weight (bone-in). For some birds, just allow a certain number of birds for each serving. **Chickens** and **Rock Cornish game hens:** about 1 pound per serving. **Turkey:** ¾ to 1 pound per serving. **Goose:** 1¼ to 1½ pounds per serving. **Duck:** 2 or 3 servings for a 4 to 5-pound bird. **Quail:** 1 serving for every 2 or 3 birds (3 to 4 oz. each). **Squab** and **chukar:** 1 serving for a ¾ to 1-pound bird. **Pheasant:** 1 serving for a 1½-pound bird; about 3 servings for a 3-pound bird.

Buying & Storing Poultry

Purchasing. When you buy fresh poultry, make sure it has been kept refrigerated, not held at room temperature. If you're purchasing prepackaged poultry (either whole or cut up), choose packages with little or no liquid in the bottom.

Good-quality whole chickens and turkeys have smooth, tight skin and plump breasts and drumsticks. Turkey should have cream-colored skin, but a chicken's skin color is no real indication of quality; color ranges from yellow to bluish-white, depending on what the bird was fed.

In choosing frozen poultry, avoid torn packages—if the bird hasn't been kept airtight, it has probably lost moisture. Also steer clear of packages containing frozen liquid. This indicates that the meat was partially thawed, then re-frozen, and may have deteriorated in quality.

Storing. *Fresh poultry is perishable and should be cooked within 3 days of purchase; if you won't use it within that time, freeze it.* Securely wrap poultry to be refrigerated in plastic wrap or butcher paper and store in the coldest part of the refrigerator. You can freeze poultry just as it comes from the market, but to prevent any chance of freezer burn, add an extra layer of insulation by enclosing the wrapped poultry in foil, heavy-duty plastic wrap, a plastic bag, or wax-coated freezer paper. Squeeze out as much air as possible before sealing, then mark the package with the type of bird, its weight, and the date. *For best results, use frozen poultry within 6 months.*

If you buy poultry complete with neck and giblets but don't want to cook them with the bird, freeze them for later use. Freeze necks, hearts, and gizzards in one container, collecting them until you have enough for stock or other purposes. Freeze livers in another container, saving them for recipes such as pâté. When you bone poultry, freeze these trimmings, too; they're good additions to the stock pot.

Thawing Frozen Poultry

For maximum retention of juices and least chance of bacterial growth, it's best to thaw all types of poultry, well wrapped, in the refrigerator. Allow 12 to 16 hours for whole chicken and 4 to 9 hours for chicken parts, depending on weight. Whole turkeys take 2 to 3 days.

If you decide to cook poultry on the spur of the moment, though, there won't be time for thawing in the refrigerator. In that case, you'll need to use another safe thawing method. You can easily defrost chicken in the microwave; just follow the guidelines on page 84. Or completely seal chicken or other small bird in a plastic bag, then submerge the bag in cold water. (The outside of the bird thaws first, and the cold water keeps the skin cool while the inside continues to thaw.) Change the water frequently so it won't get *too* cold and slow down thawing.

The cold water method also works well for turkey; except for very large birds, whole turkeys usually thaw in 5 to 8 hours. Another good method is to enclose the turkey, still in its store wrappings, in a double thickness of paper bags. Seal the bags tightly and leave the turkey at room temperature for about 8 hours. Like cold water, the bags serve as insulation, keeping the thawed parts cool until the entire bird has thawed.

It's safe to refreeze poultry (though it may lose moisture) if it has thawed only partially and ice crystals remain in the meat. But if it has thawed beyond this point, don't refreeze it; cook as soon as possible.

Boning a Chicken Breast

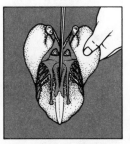 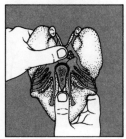

Left: Pull off skin, if desired. Lay breast skinned side down; run a sharp knife down center to sever thin membrane and expose keel bone (dark spoon-shaped bone) and thick white cartilage. **Right:** Placing one thumb on tip end of keel bone and other at base of rib cage, grasp breast firmly in both hands. Bend breast back until keel bone breaks through.

 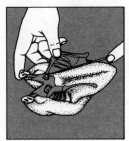

Left: Run finger under edge of keel bone and thick cartilage; then pull out and discard bone and cartilage. **Right:** Insert knife under long first rib. Resting knife against ribs, scrape meat away. Sever shoulder joint; remove ribs and attached bone. Repeat with other side of breast.

 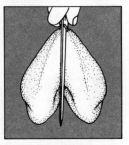

Left: Locate and remove wishbone, cutting close to bone. **Right:** Cut breast in half.

Carving a Turkey

Left: Place turkey breast up. To remove legs, cut through skin and meat between thigh and breast as shown, exposing hip joint. Then bend thigh down; cut through joint. **Right:** Cut between thigh and drumstick of each leg to expose joint; then cut through joint to sever.

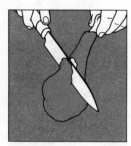

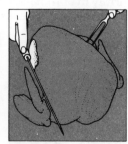

Left: To carve each drumstick, grasp tip; then thinly slice meat parallel to bone on all sides. To carve thighs, lay them flat and slice meat parallel to bone. **Right:** On each side of turkey, cut between wings and breast to expose joint; sever.

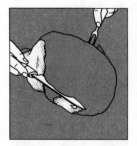

Left: On each side, cut breast horizontally just above wing joint, cutting through to ribs. **Right:** Slice meat vertically. To free meat near bone, follow contour of ribs.

Safety in Handling Poultry

In today's markets, adequate refrigeration and sanitation usually ensure high standards of freshness. But suitable hosts—such as poultry—may still carry some potentially dangerous organisms. There's no cause for worry, though; as long as you handle and store poultry properly, any organisms that may be present will be unable to produce toxins or grow to harmful proportions.

When working with raw poultry, start by rinsing the bird under cold water. After you've prepared the poultry, clean work surfaces and tools thoroughly. Soap and water followed by a good rinse are adequate for nonporous surfaces such as plastic laminate and tile; to sanitize a wooden cutting board, wash it in soapy water, then wipe with diluted chlorine bleach and rinse well with water. Composition cutting boards can simply be washed in the dishwasher.

Spoilage organisms grow best between 50°F and 130°F. At 40°F or lower, they stop growing; at 140°F, most types are killed. The greatest danger is from foods held for more than 4 hours at the prime growth temperatures. You can avoid this "danger zone" by keeping poultry cold until cooking, then promptly refrigerating any leftovers.

If left too long in a bird, stuffing provides a perfect environment for spoilage organisms. You may be tempted to get a head start by stuffing the turkey the day before, but it's best to do it just before cooking. After the bird is cooked, remove the stuffing right away and serve or refrigerate it.

Doneness Tests for Poultry

The cooking method you use determines how you'll check a bird for doneness. A test that works well for almost all types of poultry, cooked by any method, is to slash the thickest part of the meat; it should no longer look pink. (Specialty birds are an exception to this rule; see page 68.) If you're cooking both breasts and thighs, remember that the breasts cook more quickly. For extra-moist breast meat, wait to add breast pieces until 15 to 20 minutes before the end of cooking.

A meat thermometer provides the most accurate doneness test for roasted chicken or turkey. Insert it in the thickest part of the thigh (not touching bone) and roast until the thermometer registers 185°F. You can also use a meat thermometer when you're baking a whole turkey breast (cook to 170°F) or turkey thighs (cook to 185°F).

Index

METRIC CONVERSION TABLE

To change	To	Multiply by
ounces (oz.)	grams (g)	28
pounds (lbs.)	kilograms (kg)	0.45
teaspoons	milliliters (ml)	5
tablespoons	milliliters (ml)	15
fluid ounces (fl. oz.)	milliliters (ml)	30
cups	liters (l)	0.24
pints (pt.)	liters (l)	0.47
quarts (qt.)	liters (l)	0.95
gallons (gal.)	liters (l)	3.8
Fahrenheit temperature (°F)	Celsius temperature (°C)	⅝ after sub-tracting 32